Academic Advising for Student Success:
A System of Shared Responsibility

by Susan H. Frost

ASHE-ERIC Higher Education Report No. 3, 1991

Prepared by

Clearinghouse on Higher Education
The George Washington University

In cooperation with

Association for the Study
of Higher Education

Published by

School of Education and Human Development
The George Washington University

Jonathan D. Fife, Series Editor

Cite as

Frost, Susan H. 1991. *Academic Advising for Student Success: A System of Shared Responsibility.* ASHE-ERIC Higher Education Report No. 3. Washington, D.C.: The George Washington University, School of Education and Human Development.

Library of Congress Catalog Card Number 91-66412
ISSN 0884-0040
ISBN 1-878380-06-0

Managing Editor: Bryan Hollister
Manuscript Editor: Barbara Fishel, Editech
Cover design by Michael David Brown, Rockville, Maryland

The ERIC Clearinghouse on Higher Education invites individuals to submit proposals for writing monographs for the *ASHE-ERIC Higher Education Report* series. Proposals must include:
1. A detailed manuscript proposal of not more than five pages.
2. A chapter-by-chapter outline.
3. A 75-word summary to be used by several review committees for the initial screening and rating of each proposal.
4. A vita and a writing sample.

ERIC **Clearinghouse on Higher Education**
School of Education and Human Development
The George Washington University
One Dupont Circle, Suite 630
Washington, DC 20036-1183

This publication was prepared partially with funding from the Office of Educational Research and Improvement, U.S. Department of Education, under contract no. ED RI-88-062014. The opinions expressed in this report do not necessarily reflect the positions or policies of OERI or the Department.

EXECUTIVE SUMMARY

Although most college students are advised about their courses of study, few people view academic advising as a means of enhancing the positive outcomes of college. Research on college students suggests that activities like advising could increase students' involvement in their college experiences. This report focuses on outcomes of advising in the context of research on contact between faculty and students, students' involvement, and persistence. Colleges and universities could use strategic planning to design advising programs based on relationships of shared responsibility and focused on students' success. The information is appropriate for advising administrators, faculty advisers, professional advisers, peer advisers, and others who work to increase the positive outcomes of college through academic advising.

Is a New Look at Academic Advising Warranted?

Research on positive outcomes of college and on the diverse needs of students making up today's student population suggests that a new look at advising is needed. Findings link academic advising directly and indirectly to contact between faculty and students and persistence in college. For example, involvement influences learning and defines effective institutions as those having the capacity to involve students (Astin 1984). Research also indicates that frequent and meaningful contact with faculty members, especially contact focusing on intellectual or career-related issues, seems to increase students' involvement and motivation (Astin 1984; Pascarella 1980, 1985; Terenzini, Pascarella, and Lorang 1982; Tinto 1987). These results can be important to advisers, for they have the capacity to increase meaningful contact with students and to encourage them to persist in college.

One essential way to engage students in advising is to design programs that acknowledge their individual needs. Diversity not only characterizes today's student population, but also contributes to a pluralistic society that benefits all members of the college community. Because advisers can encourage students to explore their differences as positive factors, the advising relationship can be particularly responsive to pluralism. Findings of research addressing the needs of ethnic minorities, students who are academically underprepared to enter college, students with disabilities, student athletes, and international students suggest that advisers who recognize the needs of population groups and tailor advising practices appropriately engage in developmental advising. Developmental advisers involve students in the advising relationship and demonstrate that circumstances surrounding individual differences, not stereotypical differences, define students' needs.

Advisers can also respond to students who are in stages of transition. Regardless of age or personal situation, some students do not "fit" easily into college life—freshmen, students with undecided majors, transfer students, and adult students, for example. Advising freshmen is especially important. Academic integration seems to influence freshmen's development of academic skills (Tinto 1987). Advisers who facilitate assimilation to college understand factors affecting freshmen's fit and persistence. They share responsibility for advising with students and begin educational and career planning. Perceptive advisers encourage all students in transition to focus first on exploring life, career, and educational goals. Then students in transition seem better equipped to select educational programs, choose courses, and schedule classes (Tinto 1987).

What Themes Are Evident When Advising Is Considered in the Context of Research?
The central theme is one of shared responsibility, an essential ingredient in an effective relationship between adviser and student. Most students expect specific answers to short-term questions about courses, schedules, and procedures from advisers. But advising can be viewed in a broader way. Advisers who first encourage students to consider larger questions about educational and career goals and then help students plan their courses of study share responsibility for advising with students. As students frame questions about the future and seek the information they need to formulate answers, they practice behavior useful in future personal and professional situations.

Shared responsibility is also important at the institutional level. Constructing connections between academic affairs, student affairs, and support services can encourage students to become involved and to persist in college. When a broad base of the college community plans for, implements, and evaluates advising services, advising can become a systematic enterprise of the institution that enhances the educational outcomes of college.

How Can Advising Become an Essential And Systematic Enterprise?

When collaboration and shared responsibility are central to advising, an advising *system* can result. Colleges are systematic enterprises comprised of linking and interactive parts, and people and programs working together are important in achieving positive outcomes (Tinto 1987). As administrators, advising coordinators, individual advisers, and those who support advising work together, the advising program can become an essential system in the academic community. Components of the planned system are selecting, training, and recognizing advisers, and evaluating all components of the program.

What Are the Long-term Outcomes of Such an Advising System?

Ideally, advising is first a means of exploring careers and majors and then a method for selecting courses and arranging schedules. As partners in the process, students can learn to discover options, frame questions, gather information, and make decisions, which can increase their involvement in college and encourage them to persist to graduation.

Institutions as well as individuals benefit from the efforts of administrators, coordinators, advisers, and support personnel who work together to construct an advising system. When representatives from these groups plan, train for, implement, and evaluate advising, they can create a network of cooperation that can be transferred to other aspects of the college. They also model collaborative behavior for students. Program planning centered around the institution's mission and all students' needs can result in a dynamic advising system having the capacity to adapt to internal and external change.

The move from an advising system based on merely supplying answers to students' questions about scheduling and registration to a system of academic planning will not take place in one term. Nor will it take place in one academic year. The move is a deliberate, collective effort that involves changes in practices *and* attitudes. A look at the historical development of advising suggests that change is difficult at best. While some solutions to questions about broad-based approaches to advising exist, most programs still center on prescriptive activities (Habley and Crockett 1988). Even though involved students appear to be successful students, most advising programs seem to offer students short-term relationships with advisers. If the current literature on advising has one theme, it is that of shared responsibility. This theme can guide those who plan for and manage programs as well as those who interact with students. If applied creatively and with an eye to the future, perhaps academic advising relationships can provide learning experiences that prove valuable to students during the college years and beyond.

What Recommendations Can Improve Advising?

The following recommendations offer a beginning point for an advisory system based on shared responsibility. They are not intended as final solutions, but as a framework for planning and progress.

1. *Consider advising as an institutionwide system centered around students' involvement and positive college outcomes.* Advising should serve the needs of all students and contribute to their success in college.
2. *Promote concepts of shared responsibility for both students and the institution.* This orientation can serve to involve students in their academic futures and to encourage positive outcomes.
3. *Begin the advising relationship with an awareness of the larger purpose of advising and move to an awareness of details.* This approach is important for students and for institutions. Advising should contribute to students' learning and success, not merely supply answers to specific questions. It should also contribute to the overall effectiveness of education.
4. *Plan for success.* All participants in advising should be involved in an ongoing, strategic effort to center advising around a meaningful mission. Individual students reflect this orientation when they engage in academic planning with advisers.
5. *Evaluate.* Evaluation of the overall program and individual contributors is an essential part of planning; results can provide direction for change.
6. *Collaborate.* Participation in a shared advising relationship leads students to contact many members of the college community for answers to questions that arise in academic planning. These resource persons then advise both for-

mally and informally. Others support the process. Work to provide a collaborative model for students and encourage them to cooperate with their advisers.

ADVISORY BOARD

CONSULTING EDITORS

Brenda M. Albright
State of Tennessee Higher Education Commission

William E. Becker
Indiana University

Rose R. Bell
New School for Social Research

Louis W. Bender
Florida State University

Paul T. Brinkman
National Center for Higher Education Management Systems

David G. Brown
University of North Carolina–Asheville

David W. Chapman
State University of New York–Albany

Linda Clement
University of Maryland

Richard A. Couto
Tennessee State University

Peter Frederick
Wabash College

Mildred Garcia
Montclair State College

Virginia N. Gordon
Ohio State University

Wesley R. Habley
American College Testing

Edward R. Hines
Illinois State University

Dianne Horgan
Memphis State University

Don Hossler
Indiana University

John L. Howarth
Private Consultant

William Ihlanfeldt
Northwestern University

Susan Jeffords
Univesity of Washington

Greg Johnson
Harvard College

Margaret C. King
Schenectady County Community College

Christine Maitland
National Education Association

Jerry W. Miller
American College Testing

James R. Mingle
State Higher Education Executive Officers

Richard W. Moore
California State University–Northridge

Richard Morrill
Centre College

C. Gail Norris
Utah System of Education, State Board of Regents

Laura I. Rendón
North Carolina State University

Richard Robbins
State University of New York–Plattsburg

Susan Stroud
Brown University

Elizabeth Watson
California State University–Humboldt

William R. Whipple
University of Maine

Roger B. Winston
University of Georgia

REVIEW PANEL

Charles Adams
University of Massachusetts–Amherst

Richard Alfred
University of Michigan

Philip G. Altbach
State University of New York–Buffalo

Louis C. Attinasi, Jr.
University of Houston

Ann E. Austin
Vanderbilt University

Robert J. Barak
Iowa State Board of Regents

Alan Bayer
Virginia Polytechnic Institute and State University

John P. Bean
Indiana University

Louis W. Bender
Florida State University

Carol Bland
University of Minnesota

Deane G. Bornheimer
New York University

John A. Centra
Syracuse University

Arthur W. Chickering
George Mason University

Jay L. Chronister
University of Virginia

Mary Jo Clark
San Juan Community College

Shirley M. Clark
Oregon State System of Higher Education

Darrel A. Clowes
Virginia Polytechnic Institute and State University

CONTENTS

FOREWORD

High-quality academic advising is among the activities that help the most to ensure long-term success for both students and institutions. Historically, however, the full potential of academic advising has not been used—because of the often limited vision of the function of academic advising, and because of the resulting low value placed upon it by the institution in general and the faculty in particular.

When academic advising is seen chiefly as an activity to monitor a student's academic program, it typically consists of confirming that the student has taken the appropriate courses according to predetermined requirements, seeing that the student has accumulated enough credit hours to meet the minimum graduation requirements, and occasionally helping a student select a course when the "normal" courses in a program are no longer available. With such a limited custodial function, it is no wonder academic advising is given such a low relative importance.

If academic advising is assigned to a nonfaculty member, then faculty discount the results as coming from less-informed professionals at best and, more likely, from (heaven forbid) part of the administration. When faculty perform the function of academic advising, they often see it as a very unrecognized and unrewarded portion of their total activities. They often try to fulfill the responsibility as quickly as possible so that they can spend their time on more rewarding—and rewarded—activities.

When academic advising is allowed to develop a long-term connection between the academic side of an institution and the student, however, it can be a powerful force toward ensuring the student's success at the institution. The ongoing relationship established between adviser and student can engender a strong sense of understanding and appreciation that will help motivate the student. A well-designed and -operated advising office can also help guide the student through the various, ever-changing academic and social "discomfort zones" that exist between high school and college graduations.

Such a relationship can increase the effectiveness of the curriculum by helping students focus on the relationships between their life, career, and personal goals, and short- and long-term academic goals. (The importance of understanding students' goals is more fully discussed in *Student Goals for College and Courses: A Missing Link in Assessing and Improv-*

ing Academic Achievement, ASHE-ERIC Higher Education Report No. 6, 1989, by Joan S. Stark, Kathleen M. Shaw, and Malcolm A. Lowther.) And when students are more satisfied with their education, they are more likely to remain in college and support the institution.

The quality and effectiveness of the advising program at an institution can also be greatly enhanced when academic advisers systematically assess the effectiveness of their advising. This type of feedback can result in greater sensitivity to students' educational needs and lend greater validity and vitality to advising services.

This report by Susan H. Frost, director of institutional planning and research at Emory University, brings the accumulated knowledge of recent research on academic advising to the fore. Dr. Frost covers the background and current situation in academic advising, examines the effects and use of personal contact, involvement, and persistence, looks at the relationship between student and adviser, discusses the knowledge about advising a variety of student types in various situations, and offers strategies for the future success of advising programs.

For an institution to maximize its educational mission, that is, the academic success of each student, it must recognize that the student and the institution share responsibility. The vital link in this shared responsibility is the development of a long-term relationship between the student and his or her academic adviser. Through a very careful analysis of the literature, Dr. Frost has clearly developed a strategy for institutions to follow in accomplishing this goal.

Jonathan D. Fife
Series Editor, Professor, and
Director, ERIC Clearinghouse on Higher Education

ACKNOWLEDGMENTS

While writing about academic advising and positive outcomes of college, it occurred to me that my own life-long learning is a rich source of pleasure because I am fortunate to have had a number of insightful advisers. Some of them contributed to this work. The idea grew from a suggestion by Thomas G. Dyer of the University of Georgia, a former professor who continues to encourage me as a writer. Another former professor, Patrick T. Terenzini, now of Pennsylvania State University, introduced me to the concept of positive outcomes as well as to the methods for investigating their effects on students. Ronald D. Simpson of the University of Georgia extended my formal involvement in university life into perhaps one of my most valuable learning experiences. I thank all three for their careful advice.

I also thank Susan J. Daniell, Karen S. Kalivoda, Frances K. Rauschenberg, and Richard M. Rose of the University of Georgia, Thomas J. Grites of Stockton State College, Wesley R. Habley of ACT, Howard Schein of the University of Illinois, and Harry Wistrand of Agnes Scott College for their criticism of the manuscript. They and Kelley McDougal, Wanda Nicely, and Shirley Porosky of Brenau College contributed to the quality of the monograph. President John S. Burd and Vice President Margaret M. Sullivan, also of Brenau, supported the research and encouraged my continued interest in advising.

Finally, my gratitude goes to my most constant and caring advisers, Randall, Susannah, and Charles Frost. I appreciate their support, enthusiasm, and patience throughout the project and beyond.

INTRODUCTION

In view of the efforts of many colleges and universities to increase the effectiveness of their educational programs, it seems unfortunate that one process offering students the opportunity to become involved in their academic futures remains unexploited. This process is academic advising. For many students, advising is an essential, yet ineffective, part of the college experience. Traditionally, advisers help students meet institutional requirements through selection of appropriate courses. But academic advising can be viewed in a broader way. Advising can serve not only as a *method* of selecting courses but also as a *means* of achieving success for students. This dual view results from the needs of institutions and the needs of students. Colleges and universities require manageable systems to support students as they progress through the curriculum toward completion of a degree. Individuals need the support of an informed and interested representative of the institution as they identify and work toward achieving their objectives for higher education.

Advising can serve . . . as a means of achieving success for students.

Student development theory supports an individualized system of advising. Students seem to benefit from meaningful relationships with faculty members and from deliberate efforts to involve students in learning. These findings contribute both breadth and depth to concepts of advising but have not succeeded in redefining practices related to advising. To accomplish this end, administrators, advising coordinators, and individual advisers are called on to consider not only the organization of advising programs but also the opportunities afforded by advising for students and advisers to develop purposeful relationships centered on informed academic planning.

A critical look at advising practices before 1980 cautioned that advising should not be done in isolation (Grites 1979). This observation foreshadowed conclusions of national committees and survey researchers investigating higher education in America. In 1984, the National Institute of Education Study Group on the Conditions of Excellence in American Higher Education reported that students' involvement is central to learning and effective learning is a joint enterprise. Colleges that encourage active rather than passive learning and employ faculty members who are optimistic about students' potential for learning offer an enhanced undergraduate environment (Boyer 1987). These conclusions reflect the theory of students' involvement that finds direct relationships between

(1) the amount of students' learning and personal development and the quality and quantity of students' involvement and (2) the program's effectiveness and the capacity of the program to increase involvement (Astin 1984).

Academic advising can be a mechanism to involve students in learning. While successful programs take many forms, an organized agenda for advising implemented by persons responsible for routinely evaluated advising services is essential (Grites 1979). Recent reports on the condition of higher education in America underscore the timeliness of these suggestions. Both the National Institute of Education and the Carnegie Foundation for the Advancement of Teaching specifically address the importance of academic advising in their recommendations for improvements in higher education in the United States (Boyer 1987; National Institute of Education 1984).

This monograph explores advising as a contributor to students' success. When one aim of advising is to increase meaningful contact between students and advisers, students can become more involved in the academic aspects of college. Involved students are more likely to be academically and socially integrated into the college community. And integration can lead to students' persistence and success (Tinto 1975, 1987). This work is a review of the literature supporting these claims. It is not a manual for advisers, but a volume to inform advisers, advising coordinators, and administrators of advising services about research in the areas of students' success and academic advising. Findings are organized to suggest a framework for planning and delivering effective advising programs.

While faculty members, professional advisers, and peers all play essential roles in advising, most of the suggestions and recommendations that conclude this report are drawn from literature concerning students' interaction with faculty for three reasons. The first reason involves the larger body of research on the success of students. Reports of the effects of students' contact with faculty members outside the classroom lead researchers to conclude that such contacts increase the positive outcomes of college (Pascarella 1980; Pascarella and Terenzini 1976, 1978; Terenzini and Pascarella 1980; Terenzini, Pascarella, and Lorang 1982). Second, most of the literature reporting empirical research on advising concerns advising by faculty. At this time, few reports of the outcomes of advising by professional advisers, peer advisers, or others are found. Third, advising by faculty continues to be the predominant mode of delivery at all types of institutions. Fifty-three percent of 440 institutions responding to the Third American College Testing (ACT) National Survey of Academic Advising (the 1987 ACT survey) report that faculty members have sole responsibility for the delivery of advising services on their campuses. When asked for information about which of seven models of delivery best describes advising on their campuses, 88.6 percent of the respondents report using delivery systems for which faculty members have primary responsibilities for advising (Habley and Crockett 1988, p. 20). While professional advisers are being used with increasing frequency and usually advise large numbers of students, faculty members continue to advise most college students (Gordon et al. 1988). For these reasons, advising by faculty is the principal focus of this monograph. Even so, the volume is appropriate for professional advisers, peer advisers, and others. When advisers, regardless of their category, approach their assignment in ways that involve students in their academic experiences, positive outcomes can result.

After a review of the history and major developments of the last decade, the remainder of this section examines the literature concerning students' persistence and success, one approach to advising as teaching, developmental advising, and the evolution of the practice of advising.

Background

Faculty members began advising students about their courses of study when the elective system was introduced in the 1870s. The elective system, designed to improve students' lagging motivation, represented a radical departure from the prescribed curriculum of the early 19th century (Rudolph 1962). Under the new system, faculty members helped students select courses. Faculty advising was popular with students but was not always effective. As colleges grew into universities and research rivaled teaching as the major emphasis, the gap between faculty members and students widened. Students became more numerous and diverse while faculty members became more specialized. By the 1930s, most institutions had formal advising programs (Raskin 1979), but lack of faculty time and incentives led to a general weakening of the system. Academic advising was not among the student services programs initiated to meet the needs of the growing post–World War II student population. Advising was considered then, as now, primarily a function of academic affairs (Grites 1979; Habley and Crockett 1988).

In the 1960s, the large number of students applying to colleges concealed the problem. But by the 1970s, when falling enrollments and alarming attrition rates accompanied students' demands for improved advising, traditional advising programs received serious attention (see, e.g., Biggs, Brodie, and Barnhart 1975; Borgard, Hornbuckle, and Mahoney 1977; Ford 1983; Kramer and White 1982; Russel and Sullivan 1979). Important theoretical and organizational developments were also under way.

Developmental Advising: A Concept Grounded in Theory

In the 1970s, some coordinators of advising were aware of an emerging theory of student development and its potential influence on advising. They realized that advising can be a single-direction activity to select courses and plan schedules or a process of individualized teaching (Moore 1976). Theoretical developments were incorporated in a concept of advising based on the view that:

> . . . teaching includes any experience that contributes to the individual or collective growth of the community and can be evaluated. . . . The student should not be a passive receptacle of knowledge, but should share responsibility for learning with the teacher (Crookston 1972, p. 12).

The new scheme, developmental advising, was a student-centered process. Developmental advising facilitated "rational processes, environmental and interpersonal interactions, behavioral awareness, and problem-solving, decision-making, and evaluation skills" (p. 12). Within the developmental framework, advising assumed a function of teaching.

Others supported developmental advising, proposing an advising system "to help the student choose a program of study [that] will serve him in the development of his total potential" (O'Banion 1972, p. 62) and suggesting that students share responsibility for advising with the adviser and make decisions for themselves.

During this period, authors described advising as an activity at the heart of institutional action that meets students' broad educational needs. They encouraged advisers to go beyond arranging schedules and bring continuity to the experiences students encounter in the college environment. The developmental direction seemed well established (Borgard 1981; Habley 1981; Mash 1978; Raskin 1979; Shane 1981; Trombley and Holmes 1981; Walsh 1981; Winston, Ender, and Miller 1982; Winston et al. 1984).

The Evolution of Organization and Practice

Academic advising began to resemble an organized profession in the late 1970s and early 1980s. In 1979, the newly formed National Academic Advising Association (NACADA) attained a first-year membership of 500. By 1990, it had 2,450 members. Research encouraged by the association and its publications resulted in increased interest in advising. Affiliation with a national organization appeared to enhance the professional status of advisers and offered continuity to individual campus programs.

Besides NACADA, another national movement of the 1980s influenced advising practices. Organized freshman-year experience programs brought attention to all services for college freshmen, a concept that grew from the long-recognized special needs of freshmen. College presidents acknowledged those needs as early as 1910; in 1911, Reed College offered a freshman course for credit (Gordon 1989). Contemporary freshman seminars were introduced in 1972, and their popularity has grown. During academic year 1989–90, 2,187 participants attended six national and international conferences to learn about the needs of freshmen.* Proponents of structured programs for freshmen encouraged institutions to support freshmen and identified faculty as contributors to a positive campus climate. Developmental advising as a component of freshman programs seemed to enhance freshmen's success (Kramer and Spencer 1989).

National reports and results of student surveys published during the 1980s indicate that improvements in advising practices were less numerous than suggested in the literature. The National Institute of Education (1984), in its report *Involvement in Learning,* identifies advising as "one of the weakest links in the education of college students" (p. 31)

---

*Mary Stuart Hunter 1990, personal communication.

and recommends that freshmen have well-trained advisers who maintain regular contact with students. Advising is described as a college service needing improvement (Boyer 1987), and a 1985 survey conducted by the American Council on Education and the UCLA Cooperative Institutional Research Program (ACE/CIRP) confirms these opinions (Astin, Korn, and Green 1987). After two years of college, only 52.4 percent of students responding to the survey were satisfied with academic advising. After four years of college, students ranked advising services much the same. The researchers express particular concern, saying advising should be "the principal tool for helping students get involved with their studies. Involvement, in turn, is probably one of the key elements in student achievement and success" (p. 41).

Despite national attention, the influence of NACADA, and published models grounded in theory of students' development, the literature contained little to dispute the reports. In 1982, a review of more than 150 articles indicated that surveys of students' opinions dominated advising-related research (McLaughlin and Starr 1982). Few studies related techniques of advising to positive educational outcomes. Criticism of traditional practices of advising predominated, with two principal themes emerging: "Faculty members are the core of effective academic advising, and advising is an important element to student success and satisfaction in college" (p. 14). Student-opinion research continued through the 1980s (see, e.g., Fielstein 1987, 1989; Frost 1989a; Kozloff 1985; Trombley 1984), although some work to link advising to positive outcomes of college was reported (e.g., Frost 1989b, 1990b, 1991).

The 1979, 1983, and 1987 ACT surveys of academic advising provided the most comprehensive empirical research of the 1980s. While some institutions reported progress, most programs seemed to remain unfocused. For example, program evaluation doubled from 1983 to 1987, but more than half of the 1987 respondents did not evaluate advising services. The primary goal of advising in 1979 was to deliver information to students. Despite developmental advising, NACADA, and research on college students, the only 1987 goal approaching the level of "achievement satisfactory" was to provide information. The 1987 ACT survey indicated that (1) because advising remains largely unevaluated, systematic progress is difficult to determine, and (2) frequency and length of contact with an adviser can positively influence a student's perceptions of advising. Although developmental advising prevails more in theory than in practice, advisers and advising coordinators should explore the concept in training sessions (Carstensen and Silberhorn 1979; Crockett and Levitz 1983; Habley and Crockett 1988).

An Overview of the Current Situation

When compared to earlier national surveys, responses in 1987 show minimal positive change in advising services, especially in program management and evaluation and in training, evaluation, recognition and reward of advisers. Little appears to have changed at the national level (Habley 1988a). Fortunately, other indicators suggest that exemplary programs function on individual campuses. Since 1984, ACT and NACADA have joined to recognize colleges, universities, and individuals for outstanding progress in academic advising. Between 1984 and 1990, ACT and NACADA honored 45 programs and 61 advisers for exemplary advising practices.*

The conflict in attitudes toward advising on the national level and reports of actual campus practices suggest that new challenges to improve advising involve not only advising coordinators and advisers themselves, but also administrators and those who support advising programs. Research suggests that students' attitudes toward advising can influence major decisions about college. These findings are important to those who determine what resources are devoted to advising, to those who plan for and implement advising, to those who advise students, and to those who offer services that complement advising. This monograph addresses the needs of these groups.

The following section concerns positive outcomes of college, with particular emphasis on informal contacts between faculty and students, students' involvement in college, and their persistence, and addresses several questions: Is informal (or out-of-class) contact with faculty members important to students? Is involvement in college important? What is the relationship of contact and involvement to persistence? How can such positive outcomes of college be increased?

The third section explores relationships in advising. It reviews the evolution of developmental advising as a shared

---

*Wesley R. Habley 1990, personal communication.

relationship between students and advisers and addresses the following questions: Can academic advising influence contact, involvement, and persistence? Can advising be a form of teaching? How can students and advisers share responsibility for advising? How can advisers challenge students to become involved in planning their educational futures? When developmental advising is expanded to include academic planning, shared advising is likely to increase students' involvement in college. Involvement, in turn, increases the potential for the academic and social integration that can lead to persistence.

The individual needs of today's college students are explored in the fourth section. Diverse student populations— ethnic minorities, underprepared students, students with disabilities, student athletes, and international students—and students in transition—freshmen, students with undecided majors, transfer students, and adult students—are included. Characteristics and needs of these groups are discussed, considering a meaningful and manageable balance between traditional and developmental orientations of advising.

Within the context of contact, involvement, and persistence, and with an understanding of shared advising relationships and students' individual needs, a refined focus for advising is investigated in the fifth section. Planning and implementation based on research and centered on collaborative, campuswide efforts are proposed. Strategic planning methods could be used to define an advising system that includes ways to select, train, and recognize advisers and evaluate advising.

Can those who support and implement advising bring about meaningful change that will put into practice new philosophies of advising? Lasting change occurs only when the affected individuals understand the need for change and become involved in its implementation (Habley 1988a). To facilitate meaningful change, the final section discusses recommendations, conclusions, and suggestions for administrators and advising coordinators, for individual advisers, and for those who support the advising process.

CONTACT, INVOLVEMENT, AND PERSISTENCE:
Contributors to Students' Success

For the most part, successful students are involved in college and seem to find their undergraduate experiences more beneficial than do uninvolved students (Astin 1984, 1985; Boyer 1987; National Institute of Education 1984; Tinto 1975, 1987). Involvement has been perceived as an investment of energy, measured along a continuum that has quantitative (such as time) and qualitative (such as commitment) features (Astin 1984). Students' learning is directly proportional to the quantity and quality of involvement. In turn, educational effectiveness is directly related to the capacity of a policy or practice to increase students' involvement (Astin 1984). These relationships can provide direction to those who design college and university programs.

In a longitudinal investigation of factors in the college environment affecting students' persistence, academic involvement appeared to be strongly related to satisfaction with all aspects of college life except friendship with other students. Frequent interaction with faculty related more strongly to satisfaction than any other type of involvement or characteristic of the student or institution (Astin 1975, 1985). Thus, "finding ways to encourage greater student involvement with faculty (and vice versa) could be a highly productive activity on most college campuses" (Astin 1984, p. 304).

Others also acknowledge the importance of involvement (Tinto 1975, 1987). Tinto's model of students' departure is centered around the argument that voluntary withdrawal from college is a longitudinal process of interactions between the student and the academic and social systems of the college. Students' experiences with these systems continually modify their goals in ways that lead to staying or leaving (1975). Persistence "entails incorporation [or] integration . . . in the social and intellectual communities of the college" (1987, p. 126), but "more students leave their college or university prior to degree completion than stay" (1987, p. 1). Tinto predicted that over 1.6 million of the 2.6 million students entering higher education for the first time in 1986 would leave their first institution without receiving a degree and that, of those students, 1.2 million would leave higher education without graduating. Various types of contact on campus are important in causing students to persist, and interaction with faculty outside the formal boundaries of the classroom seems to be particularly significant. The secret to successful retention:

. . . lies in the willingness of institutions to involve themselves in the social and intellectual development of their students. That involvement and the commitment to students it reflects is the primary source of student commitment to the institution and their involvement in their own learning (Tinto 1987, p. 7).

The retention-involvement relationship is an important one for educators to understand (Stage 1989; Tinto 1987), for persistence increases commitment and contact with faculty is important.

Frequent faculty-student contact in and out of classes is the most important factor in student motivation and involvement. Faculty concern helps students get through rough times and keep on working (Chickering and Gamson 1987, p. 4).

But what does this observation mean for advising? Ideally, academic advisers and students meet to discuss intellectual matters, which is the subject identified by students as the most significant they face (Okun et al. 1986; Pascarella 1980; Pascarella and Terenzini 1978; Sagaria, Higginson, and White 1980; Terenzini and Pascarella 1980). Just as faculty-student contact encourages involvement and involvement leads to persistence, effective advising can increase the incidence of faculty-student contact, intensify involvement, and encourage persistence. The remainder of this section explores contact, involvement, and persistence in the context of advising, focusing on academic advising contacts and how they can contribute to involvement and persistence.

Faculty-Student Contact: A Connection to Maximize
Informal or out-of-class contact with faculty members can influence positively the outcomes of college (Hines 1981; Pascarella 1980, 1985; Terenzini and Wright 1987). Therefore, the faculty-student relationship is important to advising coordinators and advisers for at least three reasons: (1) Advising, unlike most out-of-class activities, is a service provided to most students; (2) advising provides a natural setting for out-of-class contacts with faculty to occur; and (3) advising involves intellectual matters, the most important area of concern for students. For these reasons, those responsible for

advising cannot afford to discount the influence of frequent and meaningful contact with students.

Significant positive association between informal contact with faculty and the educational aspirations, attitudes toward college, academic achievement, intellectual and personal development, and persistence of college students suggests that college programs encouraging contact between faculty and students can influence educational outcomes. In short, the most influential informal contacts between students and faculty appear to be those that extend the intellectual content of the formal academic program into the student's nonclassroom life (Pascarella 1980).

Examples of such contact include informal discussions on intellectual issues, values, or career concerns and talks about courses and academic information. While informal contact seems to contribute to both academic and personal development, encounters that extend intellectual interaction with faculty are most influential on the achievement and intellectual growth of freshmen (Pascarella 1980, 1985; Pascarella and Terenzini 1978, 1980; Terenzini and Pascarella 1980; Terenzini, Theophilides, and Lorang 1984). Because relationships inherent in academic advising provide contact based on intellectual matters, the advising setting is an important place for contacts between faulty and students to occur (Backhus 1989; Beasley-Fielstein 1986; Terenzini, Pascarella, and Lorang 1982).

While research linking contact between faculty and students to positive outcomes of college is convincing, it is not undisputed. Institutional fit, or the feeling of belonging, seems to be most important in influencing persistence and institutional commitment during the freshman year. The fit between college and student remains important during the sophomore and junior years. Furthermore, peers seem to be the most important contributors to institutional fit (Bean 1985). While students who leave a college seem less likely to have relationships with other students, they are also less likely to have relationships with faculty. Those with meaningful faculty, advising, or peer relationships are less likely to become dropouts (Cesa 1979; Flannelly and Sanford 1990).

Just as frequent informal contacts between faculty and students occur at institutions with high retention rates, institutions with low retention rates often report infrequent informal contact. Significant relationships do not develop without effort.

[Students] with meaningful faculty, advising, or peer relationships are less likely to become dropouts.

[Faculty must be] available and interested in such inter-
actions for them to occur, and conditions must be such as
to encourage those interactions when they are desired by
faculty and students. Though behaviors may be important
. . . those interactions outside the classroom . . . eventually
shape student decisions regarding departure (Tinto 1987,
p. 66).

Students identify inadequate advising as a significant factor
in their decisions to leave college. On the other hand, the
positive attitudes of faculty and staff seem to be the strongest
contributors to students' success (Astin, Korn, and Green
1987; Beal and Noel 1980; Tinto 1987).

Involvement and Persistence: Positive Outcomes of College

Others investigate the behavior of students on deeper levels;
they not only consider the importance of contact but also
relate persistence to students' involvement, academic and
social integration, motivation, and satisfaction with educational quality (see, e.g., Flannelly and Sanford 1990; Okun
et al. 1986; Pascarella and Terenzini 1981; Sagaria, Higginson,
and White 1980; Stage 1989; Terenzini and Wright 1987; Tinto
1987). Researchers conclude that involved students invest
energy in the academic experience, participate in campus
activities, interact frequently with faculty, staff, and peers,
and are more likely to remain in college (Astin 1984, 1985;
Tinto 1987).

Contact can be linked to involvement and persistence both
directly and indirectly. Research suggests that the experiences
of students after they enroll in college might be more important than their precollege attributes, that efforts to enhance
persistence should concentrate on the experiences of students
after beginning college, and that academic integration might
be more important than social interaction in influencing the
development of academic skills and persistence. Thus, the
quality and impact of informal contact between faculty and
students could be as important as frequency of contact to
involvement and persistence (Pascarella and Terenzini 1980;
Terenzini and Pascarella 1978; Terenzini and Wright 1987).

The reasons students give for leaving a college indicate that
dissatisfied students appear to be "discouraged" (Janasiewicz
1987); often they are confused about their options, unsuc-

cessful in the classroom, and likely to withdraw from school. Such students could be among those who consistently give advising low ratings on national surveys and prompt the conclusion that:

> . . . *although students generally report high levels of satisfaction with their college experience . . . there is much that colleges and universities can do to enhance learning opportunities, . . . to provide more and better assistance in a range of nonclassroom (but not necessarily nonacademic) services, and to retain students* (Astin, Korn, and Green 1987, p. 42).

When considered together, conclusions about contact, involvement, and persistence have powerful implications for advising coordinators, for individual advisers, and for students. Advising is sometimes the only structured relationship that links students with concerned representatives of the institution. Within the boundaries of the relationship, it is possible to increase meaningful contact with faculty, help students become involved in their academic experiences, and encourage students to remain in college—desirable outcomes for students and for institutions. They suggest that the potential influence of academic advising is profound.

The next section explores advising relationships in the context of contact, involvement, and persistence and the needs of specific groups of college students, investigating strategies for planning, implementing, and evaluating campus advising programs.

THE ADVISING RELATIONSHIP: Students And Advisers Sharing Responsibility

The value of the relationship between adviser and student, when considered in the context of contact, involvement, and persistence, seems evident. A number of authors espouse a shared relationship; recent empirical research indicates that the preferences of students and advisers are addressed when each participates in fulfilling the requirements of an advising relationship (Frost 1990b). Such approaches to advising are centered around the needs of students, not the needs of colleges (Dassance and Batdorf 1980) and suggest that advising is more meaningful when viewed as a *teaching process,* not as a product.

Academic planning, though usually addressed indirectly, is becoming an integral part of the process of orienting students to change and encouraging them to accept responsibility for their educational futures (Frost 1989a; Gish and Dentler 1989). When planning becomes part of the developmental advising relationship, students practice skills they can use throughout life. This section explores developmental advising and academic planning. A combined approach should be adopted for a shared advising relationship.

Developmental Advising: A Teaching Process

Historically, the goal of advising was to help students choose classes and register for classes. Those decisions then became central points around which students selected majors and organized their lives. But a new component was added to the concept of advising in the early 1970s (Crookston 1972). By linking advising to the theory of student development, advising could be viewed as a form of teaching. This concept of advising was organized around two principles: (1) Higher learning provides an opportunity for developing persons to plan to achieve self-fulfilling lives, and (2) teaching includes any experience that contributes to individual growth and can be evaluated. "The student should not be a passive receptacle of knowledge, but should share responsibility for learning with the teacher" (Crookston 1972, p. 12).

A new definition of advising was proposed within this framework. First, traditional, or prescriptive, advising is a relationship acknowledging the authority of advisers and the limitations of students. During the advising period, prescriptively advised students bring problems about courses and registration to advisers for solutions. Advisers supply answers to spe-

cific questions but rarely address broad-based academic concerns (Crookston 1972; Gordon 1988).

Developmental advising, the term for the new approach, suggests that students and advisers share responsibility for advising. It contributes to students' rational processes, environmental and interpersonal interactions, behavioral awareness, and problem-solving, decision-making, and evaluation skills. The *relationship* between adviser and student is vital. Long-term as well as immediate goals are important. When viewed in this way, advising becomes a teaching function.

Developmental advising was later described as "the vehicle most likely to succeed" in providing a personalized education (Gordon 1988, p. 108). Developmental advising can encourage students to use the cognitive and affective domains as they make academic, career, and moral decisions. Developmental advisers can create a sense of friendliness for students and encourage them to explore life and career goals, solve problems, and make educational decisions. Students who are developmentally advised usually spend more time involved in the advising process than do students who are traditionally advised. Even though advisers and students spend relatively little time together, students seek help from department chairs, instructors, career planners, and other students taking courses or majoring in areas that interest them. These problem-solving activities not only provide answers to questions about courses and schedules, but can also help students develop thinking skills (Carberry, Baker, and Prescott 1986; Ender, Winston, and Miller 1982; Frost 1989a, 1989b, 1990b, 1991; Gordon 1988; Habley and Crockett 1988; Thomas and Chickering 1984).

Theory Supports the Concept

Advising as a *process* focuses attention on students' interaction with the higher education enterprise, not simply on their courses of study. Specific principles of developmental theorists (e.g., Havighurst et al., cited in Miller and McCaffrey 1982, p. 20) support the concept of developmental advising. These scholars describe human development as a cumulative process that follows a simple-to-complex continuum in an orderly and stage-related manner. Although not a straight line progression, development continues regardless of age and is influenced by previous occurrences in life. One grows and changes as new experiences are added. Thus, growth is characterized by common processes, not specific content (Isakson, Lawson, and MacArthur 1987; Miller and McCaffrey 1982).

Academic advisers who demonstrate an understanding of these principles can stimulate the development of their students. Many components of advising are based on psychosocial theory (Chickering 1969). The college years are a time of considerable change, and college students' developmental tasks can be organized into seven vectors: developing competence, managing emotions, developing autonomy, establishing identity, freeing interpersonal relationships, developing purpose, and developing integrity (Chickering 1969). The three key vectors for delivering academic advising are the following:

- *Developing competence,* or increasing the intellectual, physical, and social skills that lead to the knowledge that one is capable of handling and mastering a range of tasks;
- *Developing autonomy,* or confronting a series of issues leading ultimately to the recognition of one's independence; and
- *Developing purpose,* or assessing and clarifying interests, educational and career options, and lifestyle preferences and using these factors to set a coherent direction for life (Gordon 1988, p. 109).

A number of attributes of effective advising programs contribute to definitions of developmental advising. The following attributes affect primarily students and advisers:

- *Developmental advising is a process,* not a paper-endorsing activity. It is a continuous and cumulative relationship with both direction and purpose.
- *Developmental advising is concerned with human growth.* The cognitive, affective, career, physical, and moral areas are all legitimate concerns; personal goals and objectives are important considerations.
- *Developmental advising is goal related.* Goals are collaboratively established to provide direction for planning academic, career, and personal growth.
- *Developmental advising requires establishment of caring interaction.* The adviser is a role model who is responsible for the initial advising relationship, but both parties contribute to sustaining it (Ender, Winston, and Miller 1982, pp. 7–8).

Other conditions concern the organization of developmental advising within the institution:

- *Developmental advising is a collaborative effort between academic affairs and student affairs.* Effective programs join the expertise of faculty and student affairs professionals for maximum benefits to students.
- *Developmental advising uses all resources of the academic community.* Although advisers serve as the hub of students' learning experiences, they do not possess expertise in all areas. Students seek out other faculty members and campus resources as they move through the educational planning process (Ender, Winston, and Miller 1982, pp. 7–8).

Advising Preferences: What Do Students And Advisers Want?

During the 1980s, definitions of developmental advising were refined. Students and advisers seem to agree on the responsibilities of the advisee and the adviser but want specific expectations of each to be identified (Larsen and Brown 1983). Problem-solving and goal-setting strategies are important to students as they decide on academic majors. They seem to prefer advisers who assist with the selection of classes but allow students to make decisions, get to know students beyond their test scores or grades, relate advising to the choice of major or career, and are knowledgeable about all aspects of the institution (Winston and Sandor 1984).

In a later rating of developmental and prescriptive advising, students preferred a list of prescriptive items. While desiring a personal relationship with the adviser, they preferred not to discuss family or peers. They favored advisers who provide academic information related to requirements for graduation, selecting courses, planning a course of study, and exploring career options. On close examination, these results seem to complement rather that conflict with prior work. Students appear to want an individual advising relationship, but one organized around academic matters and not personal concerns. Findings support the dual role of advising and suggest that students differentiate the functions of academic advisers from those of personal counselors (Fielstein 1987, 1989).

Developmental advisers appear to favor similar activities. Faculty members rated as developmental advisers by their students divide advising activities into three classifications: (1) activities that concern personal attitudes and experiences related to college; (2) activities that concern group programs, policies, and opportunities; and (3) maintenance activities, such as signing forms, selecting courses, and planning schedules. Most developmental advisers routinely discuss vocational activities with students and refer them to campus resources when appropriate. Developmental advisers make special efforts to encourage students to become involved in college experiences and discuss with students their academic progress (Frost 1990a, 1990c). They usually do not act as personal counselors but identify counseling needs and refer students to appropriate campus resources when appropriate.

Although authors recommend developmental advising (see, e.g., Carberry, Baker, and Prescott 1986; Frost 1989a; Habley 1981; Kapraun and Coldren 1982; Kramer et al. 1987; Thomas and Chickering 1984; Wooldridge 1982), few campuses have implemented the concept. Advising is still perceived as a low-status function that addresses the information needed by students rather than contributing to their development (Habley and Crockett 1988). While advising at the national level seems to have changed very little in the last decade, however, important progress is occurring on campuses:

In 15 years, individual campuses have moved from the point of awareness to the point of implementation and evaluation of significant enhancements in advising programs. . . . These accomplishments form the true basis for optimism for it is on the campus level where students, the direct beneficiaries of quality advising, are served (Habley 1988a, p. 8).

Increased contact between faculty and students and students' involvement in educational processes are basic components of developmental advising. Although developmentally advised students do not spend inordinate amounts of time in formal advising sessions, they are more likely to meet informally with their advisers and seek out other faculty members and campus resources to gather information and plan their academic futures. These activities can increase students' involvement in the college community (Frost 1989b, 1990b). Despite its consistently low rating for satisfaction among students, advising is "probably the principal tool for helping students get involved in their studies" (Astin, Korn, and Green

Students appear to want an individual advising relationship, but one organized around academic matters and not personal concerns.

1987, p. 40). Proponents of developmental advising suggest that advisers and advising coordinators direct greater attention to true developmental objectives (Habley 1988a).

Academic Planning: Practice for the Future

Academic planning is an extension of the concept of developmental advising. Development can occur as the result of a planned educational program (Kohlberg and Mayer 1979). It follows that participation in planning, with the accompanying tasks of identifying a mission and objectives, considering alternatives, and arriving at an informed decision, can be a growth experience for students. Planning implies involvement. When advisers encourage students to plan by asking open-ended questions about students' futures, their majors, and selection of courses, they encourage students to become involved in their academic futures (Frost 1990a). When students engage in academic planning with advisers, students can become full partners in a shared relationship.

In any setting, properly structured plans can guide decision making, encourage an awareness of external factors that influence the future, and bring focus to specific goals (Cope 1981). Planning as applied to academic advising not only assists students in making immediate academic choices, but also contributes to the teaching role of advising by serving as a model for future behavior. In this time of professional mobility and diverse career paths, positive orientation to change and the skills to manage change are valuable.

Advisers might consider the following observations when planning with students:

1. Students' plans are always subject to change, especially in today's diverse society.
2. A primary function of planning is to help students cope with positive change by learning to analyze and synthesize.
3. A reasonable academic planning model represents a spiral approach rather than a fragmented, linear approach. Students need accurate information to make informed choices, they need encouragement and sometimes advocacy, and they need to identify goals, consider options, deal with obstacles, and set realistic time lines. With the spiral approach, students determine the sequence of events; any starting point can become a point of departure.

4. Students deserve the best thinking of faculty and staff regarding the larger educational issues that underlie their questions and perplexities. Advisers who talk to students about acquiring content versus methodology or process, obtaining a credential versus obtaining an education, generalization versus specialization, and faculty versus student responsibility for learning should be successful (Mahoney 1982, p. 72).

Developmental advising is a relationship that focuses on the needs of students. Successful advisers are aware of the characteristics of specific groups of students and how these characteristics can influence the need for advising. Successful advisers encourage students' involvement through academic planning. The following section considers the characteristics and needs of students making up today's diverse student population and addresses several questions: What groups of students have special advising needs? What are the characteristics of these groups that determine their advising needs? How can advisers address these needs and encourage all students to share responsibility for academic planning?

FOCUSING THE ADVISING RELATIONSHIP:
Attention to Students' Needs

Diversity characterizes today's college population. Students who are members of one or more population groups "reflect the pluralism of our country" (Green 1989, p. 29) that benefits all campus constituents. They also bring special needs to the advising relationship. Some students have special advising needs not because they are members of special populations, but because they are in stages of transition. Advisers who view students as individuals can encourage them to see their differences as positive factors (Saunders and Ervin 1984). Advising coordinators can provide the training advisers need to address the needs of individual students effectively.

What Are the Differences that Matter?
Identification of campus population groups is a first step in understanding the needs of different students. Advisers who recognize these groups and tailor advising practices appropriately engage in a developmental process. They demonstrate that circumstances surrounding individual differences, not stereotypical differences, define individual needs. Some special students seem hesitant to ask for the services they require because of their distinctive status. This hesitancy can contribute to academic difficulty and cause students to leave higher education without adjusting to college life (Tinto 1987). Interested and informed advisers who assist students as they become contributing members of the academic community can encourage special populations to remain in college. Research addresses the needs of many groups characterized by diversity. This monograph discusses in detail the advising needs of ethnic minorities, academically underprepared students, students with disabilities, student athletes, and international students. Table 1 summarizes characteristics of the groups and effective advising techniques for each group.

Ethnic minorities
In the 1980s, the U.S. population growth rate was at a historic low point, yet minority populations grew at two to fourteen times the corresponding nonminority population. While the proportion of minorities in the population is increasing, minorities, with the exception of Asian-Americans, remain underrepresented among college students. Because the elevated growth rate of minority populations is largely the result of greater numbers of young people, the change has signifi-

TABLE 1

DIVERSE POPULATIONS: SUMMARY OF CHARACTERISTICS AND TECHNIQUES FOR ADVISING

	Ethnic Minorities	Academically Underprepared Students
Characteristics Important to Advisers	• Declining percentages of African-Americans and Hispanics enrolling • Often have low self-concept, few positive expectations • Academic performance related to satisfaction with college • Achievement appears to be a problem of preparation, not of race • Lack of role models on campus	• Increasing participation in college • Often dependent learners with low self-concept • Many deficient in basic skills • Need to experience academic success • Hesitant to seek needed support services
Advising Techniques	• Make efforts to enhance the college-student fit • Encourage their involvement on campus • Suggest campus resources when needed • Encourage positive self-concept • Avoid stereotypical attitudes and expectations • Suggest academic experiences that can prove successful, especially at first • Acknowledge the importance of role models	• Establish a trusting advising relationship • Begin with intrusive advising techniques • Discuss the purposes of college early in the relationship • Encourage development of basic skills first • Recommend intervention programs and campus resources when needed

Students with Disabilities	Student Athletes	International Students
• Increasing participation in college	• Many underprepared academically	• Increasing numbers of traditional age
• One or more major life activities limited	• Many have unrealistic career goals	• Most from Third World countries
• Prefer to see themselves as "able" rather than "disabled"	• Often academically unsuccessful if unsupported	• Academic and career concerns primary
• Expressed need for removal of barriers to full participation	• Some must comply with external and team regulations	• Need practical experience in career areas
• Need support from peers and others		• Concerned with language difficulties, financial problems, and selecting relevant programs
		• Non-Western students see instructors as revered authorities
• Understand students' abilities and the barriers they face	• Begin support services with entering freshmen	• Be prepared to translate collegiate and U.S. culture
• Display positive attitudes about the integration of students into the college community	• Be aware of the constraints of participation in athletics	• Be familiar with students' academic preparation
• Encourage full participation in college	• Establish academic support and intervention systems	• Focus on designing academic plans that are relevant to home country of student
• Recommend support services when needed	• Teach problem-solving and decision-making skills	• Encourage open view about U.S. lifestyles
• Act as an advocate for special and campus resources	• Encourage academic commitment equal to athletic commitment	• Encourage involvement in college community

cance for higher education. Despite growth, fewer numbers of minority students are enrolling in colleges and universities ("Minority Access" 1987; Richardson and Bender 1987; Richardson and de los Santos 1988).

Enrollment of African-Americans exhibits the most serious decline in college attendance, but data about Hispanic students are no more encouraging. While their numbers have grown, Hispanics remain the most underrepresented major ethnic group in college. Eventually, higher education must address problems of minority access. As enough majority students will not be available to fill the nation's colleges and universities, the long-term futures of some institutions could depend on their abilities to attract and retain minority students (Estrada 1988; "Hispanic Students" 1988; "Minority Access" 1987; Richardson and de los Santos 1988).

Retention and achievement of minority students are major concerns for many colleges and universities. Minority students often enter college unprepared to meet the academic and social demands of their new environment. Before they can be successful in the classroom, they must adjust socially and academically. Because minority students often have less support from their home environments during the adjustment period than do nonminority students, a supportive college community that provides an appropriate balance of challenge and support seems essential (Cibik and Chambers 1991; Hughes 1987; McCauley 1988; McPhee 1990; Mallinckrodt 1988; Williams and Leonard 1988). A supportive community is one in which students have opportunities for friendship, participation in the life of the campus, and a sense of progress and success in their academic pursuits (Fleming 1984). Successful minority students seem to understand the historical context through which their access to college was achieved. They learn to act as advocates for themselves and develop a cultural identity within the college community (Astin et al. 1982; Wright 1984).

Some African-American students demonstrate a lack of self-confidence and fail to recognize their academic deficiencies. They also experience more difficulty in setting goals and receive less positive reinforcement for their accomplishments than do white students. African-American students who make plans seem to be more successful in college than those who do not plan; those with low aspirations and vague plans are likely to leave school (Astin 1975; Bohn 1973; Sedlacek 1987).

Studies of predominately black and predominately white institutions indicate that for African-American and for white students, academic performance is strongly related to satisfaction with college, high levels of campus involvement, and positive relationships with faculty members. Yet African-American students on white campuses are significantly less involved than white students and are less likely to report positive relationships with faculty members (Allen 1988; Crosson 1988). These findings suggest that advising could "form the bridge between individual dispositions and institutional tendencies; together these factors determine student outcomes" (Allen 1988, pp. 411–12).

Meaningful faculty contact is no less critical for Hispanic students:

> *Scratch a Hispanic student and you'll probably find someone in his or her background who showed a special interest in them, who took them aside and gave them the aspiration and encouragement to go on to higher education* (Fiske 1988, p. 31).

Because a close family relationship is a strength of their culture, Hispanic freshmen often find leaving home and adjusting to college more difficult than do majority or other minority students. They naturally seek advisers and faculty members to guide them yet are not assertive about identifying their needs (Fiske 1988).

Positive expectations and experiences with role models often help minority students persist in college. While attrition of minority, especially African-American, students seems the result primarily of a lack of academic integration (Donovan 1984; Eddins 1982), positive self-concept, realistic appraisal of academic skills, familiarity with institutional policies, and the development of academic skills can influence academic success (Nettles and Johnson 1987; Pounds 1989; Tracey and Sedlacek 1985). This evidence suggests that for freshmen minority students, academic advising can be especially important. Advisers can meet critical needs by encouraging a positive self-concept and avoiding all stereotypical solutions to academic problems. They can also help students get to know the academic community by introducing them to student support services and other resources.

Although students perceive minority role models as positive influences and research indicates that an intellectual role model is the "single most important element of ethnic minority student retention" (Walton 1979), minority faculty members are scarce on most campuses (Fiske 1988). To ease this problem, advising coordinators should consider recruiting minorities to serve as advisers for minority and majority students. Other advisers can be trained to meet the needs of minorities by encouraging involvement and frequent contact between faculty and students.

Minority students are often academically underprepared for college. Therefore, advisers of minority students can benefit not only from general recommendations for an improved college experience for minorities, but also from suggestions about students' achievement as well. Advisers who encourage minority students to pursue challenging courses of study congruent with their abilities and goals can avoid stereotyping their students. For all minority students, the college-student "goodness of fit" is important. Advisers who discuss "fit" with students can help them make sound decisions about academic programs. In addition to advising, however, many minority students also seem to need support groups, tutoring, and counseling about careers. Those providing such support should be reminded to work collaboratively with advisers to enhance the achievement of minority students (Green 1989; Grites 1982; Richardson and de los Santos 1988; Richardson, Simmons, and de los Santos 1987; Williams and Leonard 1988).

Academically underprepared students

Research suggests that the two strongest predictors of success in college are high school grade point average (GPA) and scores on college admission tests (Astin, Korn, and Green 1987). These findings, coupled with indications that increasing numbers of college freshmen demonstrate deficiencies in one or more basic skill areas and that 82 percent of all institutions and 94 percent of public institutions offer at least one course considered remedial in nature (U.S. Dept. of Education 1985), imply that retaining academically underprepared students presents a special challenge for advisers. Underprepared students generally have deficiencies that make it difficult to achieve what has been identified as their college objective. Certain characteristics contribute to their high-risk status. Many underprepared students seem to lack basic skills in language, writing, and computation and study habits. Some have unfocused career objectives, are unmotivated, expect to fail, and do not graduate. Underprepared students need skills that allow them to achieve on the same levels as students who are adequately prepared. They also need to expect and experience success. Just as diversity characterizes the general student population, it characterizes underprepared college students; they can be students of traditional college age, returning adults, athletes, or international students. Many are freshmen. They might be disabled. They come from varying socioeconomic backgrounds. Most underprepared students have made choices at some time that contributed to their lack of readiness for college. In their cases, mere enrollment can signal a willingness to begin to change the directions of their futures (Grites 1982; Hardin 1988; Noel et al. 1985; Walter 1982).

Not all advising techniques are effective for all academically deficient students, but for most, a trusting student-adviser relationship can be a first step toward success. The advising *relationship* is critical. Most underprepared students enter college as dependent learners and display deficiencies that impede their achievement and contribute to a sense of failure. Generally, they lack confidence and hesitate to seek available support. Advisers who encourage underprepared students to view themselves as having control over their chances of success can help them become independent learners. Then these students can begin to take responsibility for their academic futures (Wooldridge 1982).

Intrusive advising can be particularly useful to advisers who want to help underprepared students remain in college.

To improve both verbal and nonverbal communication skills is a first step to enabling students to interact successfully with advisers, instructors, peers, and employers and to become independent learners. Later, they can acquire cognitive and problem-solving skills. Advisers can begin the learning process by discussing the purposes of a college education and encouraging students to explore various academic services. Then advisers can address specific academic needs. In many cases, advisers of underprepared students should consider assuming responsibility for sustaining the advising relationship at first by contacting students frequently and encouraging them to succeed (Grites 1982; Scherer and Wygant 1982).

Intrusive advising, or "deliberate intervention . . . to enhance student motivation" (Earl 1988, p. 27), can contribute to success for students in academic difficulty. Begun out of concern for freshmen and sophomores who were unsuccessful in college, intrusive advising employs some prescriptive advising tools. Intrusive advisers encourage students to seek academic assistance as soon as the students think they need it. Thus, advisers address the developmental goal of teaching students to solve problems. Motivation is the primary focus of intrusive advising. Ideally, students in academic difficulty who are intrusively advised seek support even before the institution has identified them as "in trouble" (Earl 1988).

Intrusive advising can be particularly useful to advisers who want to help underprepared students remain in college. Certain principles identify intrusive advising:

1. Academic and social integration are the keys to the persistence of freshmen in college (Earl 1988).
2. Deficiencies in this integration can be treated. Students can be taught the skills they need through intrusive advising (Glennen and Baxley 1985).
3. Students' motivation is not the cause but the result of intrusive intervention (Earl 1988).

In some programs, probationary students who are intrusively advised attend sessions to explore the causes of their academic difficulties. They then agree to specific courses of action and continue to meet with advisers to monitor progress. A final meeting to discuss current grades and plan courses for the following grading period concludes the intrusive contact. This pattern seems to result in higher grades and increased retention for those students who enter the process because of academic difficulty (Earl 1988; Lyons 1985; Taylor et al. 1987).

Many underprepared students enter college with inappropriately defined academic and career goals that impede their success. They might need a combination of advising and continuing academic intervention programs, such as the development of basic skills and study skills, and career counseling. Most intervention courses meet throughout the freshman year and contribute to an increased GPA and student retention. Usually advisers refer students to such support services; in time, students learn to identify problems for themselves and initiate services before they reach the crisis stage (Lyons 1985; Patrick, Furlow, and Donovan 1988).

Like some minority students, underprepared students often are unaccustomed to success. Effective advisers help such students increase their chances of success by encouraging them to investigate their strengths. Then underprepared students can select courses, programs of study, and careers that employ these strengths. Advisers often direct these students to specific campus resources for assistance with study skills and exploration of various careers. Above all, they help underprepared students integrate out-of-class and in-class learning experiences.

Students with disabilities

Section 504 as amended of the federal Rehabilitation Act of 1973 protects the rights of persons with disabilities. The law states that persons with disabilities shall not "be excluded from participation in, be denied the benefits of, or be subjected to discrimination under any program or activity receiving federal financial assistance." Section 504 defines the protected person as "any person who has a physical or mental impairment [that] substantially limits one or more major life activities. . . ."

The college population protected by Section 504 increased from 2.7 percent in 1978 to 7.7 percent in 1985 (Ivory 1986) and continues to grow. While some disabilities are identified easily because they are visible, other severe and limiting disabilities are invisible. To serve all students protected by Section 504, colleges and universities are being called on to create "an environment conducive to equal opportunity by educating college and university personnel on disability-related issues" (Kalivoda and Higbee 1989, p. 15).

While significant efforts to provide services without altering the quality of educational programs are under way, types of support vary. Larger and public institutions most often employ support staff to serve students with disabilities; community colleges usually offer broad-based institutional support. Most institutions are taking steps to remove architectural and attitudinal barriers to full participation in the college program (Kalivoda and Higbee 1989; Marion and Iovacchini 1983).

Although modest amounts of research exist concerning the special advising needs of students with disabilities, the advising relationship can be especially important. In initial advising sessions, advisers who display an understanding of the barriers students with disabilities face can provide early individualized support. Among these barriers are:

1. Attitudinal barriers, such as the attitudes of faculty and fellow students that create obstacles to academic and/ or social integration;
2. Policy barriers, such as institutional rules regulating the use of readers and library materials for visually impaired students, placement of auditory telephones on campus for hearing-impaired students, or the presence and placement of emergency care for students with unseen disabilities, such as epilepsy, diabetes, or asthma;
3. Social barriers, such as not allowing persons with physical disabilities to be accompanied to social or sports events by attendants or not providing special orientation services to address the needs of these students; and
4. Architectural barriers, such as the absence of ramps, designated parking, curb cuts, suitable living areas, or elevators.

Because needs for access vary, students with disabilities deal with barriers to full participation in different ways.

Despite society's view of persons with disabilities as "unable," most students with disabilities see themselves as "able." Consequently, students prefer a supportive college environment and accessible information about opportunities available to them rather than offers of emotional support (Kalivoda and Higbee 1989; Kriegsman and Hershenson 1987; Shell, Horn, and Severs 1988; Stilwell, Stilwell, and Perritt 1983).

Like their peers without disabilities, students with disabilities are concerned about gaining intellectual and social competence, establishing and maintaining relationships, and deciding on careers and life-styles. While students with disabilities have the same needs for academic and social integration as students without disabilities, instructors are sometimes uncertain about how to interact with them. This uncertainty can lead to anxiety for the instructor and contribute to an unwelcome environment. Helpful faculty members display positive attitudes toward integrating students with disabilities into the normal classroom and willingly adjust assignments and testing situations to allow access without sacrificing quality. Research suggests that women instructors, instructors who are self-assured rather than apprehensive about interacting with students with disabilities, instructors in education and the social sciences, and instructors with previous experience teaching students with disabilities are effective instructors for students with physical disabilities (Fonosch and Schwab 1981; Hameister 1989; McQuilkin, Freitag, and Harris 1990; Wiseman, Emry, and Morgan 1988).

A growing subgroup of students with disabilities are students with identified learning disabilities. This population is diagnosed more often now than in the past. Approximately 14 percent of students with disabilities have learning disabilities, a tenfold increase in identification since 1978. Students with learning disabilities seem to benefit from strategies to enhance their skills in taking notes and tests, classes that proceed according to a preannounced calendar and carefully prepared syllabus, and supportive handouts from instructors. Testing can present challenges for instructors who are not trained to assess students with learning disabilities. All faculty members can benefit from orientation to services for students with learning disabilities and to the legal guidelines protecting them (McGuire and O'Donnell 1989).

Advisers and instructors might find helpful a number of general guidelines offered by those who coordinate services for students with disabilities. Students with disabilities are like other students except for the special limitation(s) imposed by their disabilities. They want others to respect the rights of students with disabilities to ask for help, speak directly to them, and offer assistance only if asked or if the need is obvious. Students with disabilities have varying lifestyles, attitudes, and personality characteristics, just as do students without disabilities. It is important to appreciate these students' *abilities.* They often experience difficulties stemming more from society's attitudes and barriers than from their disabilities (Kalivoda, Young, and Wahlers 1989, pp. 7–8).

While academic advisers are not responsible for classroom practices or institutional policy, advisers of students with disabilities can contribute to their advisees' integration into the college community, direct them to needed services, and assist in selecting classes. Advisers can encourage students with disabilities to participate in the advising relationship by discussing their strengths. Then advisers can more effectively guide students with disabilities into courses of study that challenge their abilities and provide viable career opportunities.

Advisers who let students know about less-than-ideal situations in their own lives seem to offer a welcoming environment. Successful advisers of students with disabilities:

> . . . can learn to communicate to their advisees that . . . they have also experienced difficult problems, have learned to cope, are equal as human beings, have the capacity to care, and have the capacity for empathy (Paulsen 1989, p. 9).

In addition to helping students with disabilities participate fully in college, advisers have the opportunity to act as advocates for these students. They can encourage attitudes, practices, and campus networks that enable students with disabilities "to achieve maximum independence, enhanced self-esteem, and full participation in the pursuit of higher education" (Kalivoda and Higbee 1989, p. 21).

Student athletes

Findings regarding the academic, social, and personal development of student athletes present "divergent and contrary" information about the outcomes of athletic participation during college (Ryan 1989, p. 123). In some cases, athletes score significantly lower than nonathletes in educational and career plans, with athletic participation appearing to be especially detrimental for men in National Collegiate Athletic Association (NCAA) Division I schools. Women athletes appear more intrinsically motivated to pursue athletics and encounter fewer academic problems than do men athletes. Other findings, however, suggest that athletic involvement enhances persistence, overall satisfaction with the college experience, motivation to earn a degree, the development of interpersonal skills, and leadership abilities (Astin 1984; Blann 1985; McLaughlin 1986; Ryan 1989; Sowa and Gressard 1983).

A number of factors influence the academic performance of student athletes:

1. The time devoted to daily practice
2. The degree of inflexibility regarding time and location
3. General fatigue resulting from practice and play
4. Participation in "study" aspects of the sport
5. College majors that are precluded because of practice schedules and

6. The challenge to student athletes to find a reasonable balance between athletics and academics (Kramer 1986a, p. 67).

Although most recommendations for assisting student athletes involve academic advising, specific programs, delivery systems, and evaluation of services are not documented (McLaughlin 1986).

The need for academic support of student athletes at all levels of competition appears well defined. Most male and female athletes enter college with slightly lower GPAs and standardized test scores than their peers who are not athletes. African-American athletes have lower scores than white athletes. While varsity competition does not seem detrimental to the academic performance of student athletes admitted normally, those admitted with weak high school preparation earn lower GPAs in college than their peers admitted normally (Ervin et al. 1985; Gurney and Stuart 1987; McLaughlin 1986; Purdy, Eitzen, and Hufnagel 1982). When considered in the context of commitments of nonnegotiable time and energy, well-structured academic support seems essential for success.

Intervention similar to the intrusive advising found successful for freshmen can be useful for at-risk athletes. Highly structured advising encourages athletes to develop appropriate academic behavior and serve as role models for their peers. It is important for advisers of at-risk athletes to suggest intervention strategies early in their college careers, to involve coaches and other athletic officials in the academic world of athletes, and to be sources of emotional support. While athletes should show progress toward the degree, carefully planned course schedules for the quarters of athletic participation can contribute to higher GPAs (Ender 1983). Because many student athletes are likely to be undecided about their major field of study, they might benefit from the decision-making processes of a developmental advising relationship (Gordon 1984).

Unlike other special populations, student athletes who participate in sports at NCAA Division I member institutions must comply with academic guidelines established outside the college or university. Division I student athletes must meet the requirements for high school GPA and entering test scores specified by the NCAA or delay athletic participation for one academic year (Schubert and Schubert 1983). These regulations have resulted in extensive media and institutional review of the eligibility of Division I student athletes. Prompted by numerous violations, many colleges and universities recognize their ethical responsibilities to offer at-risk student athletes positive academic support and intervention programs. Such programs can improve the GPAs and persistence rates of athletes. Conversely, student athletes not supported in academically competitive institutions are often unsuccessful in the classroom (American College 1984; Gurney and Johnston 1986).

In 1975, advisers of athletes organized to help student athletes maintain their eligibility and achieve graduation (Downing 1981). The resulting organization, the National Association of Academic Advisors for Athletics (NAAAA), seeks to support and enhance the academic achievement of intercollegiate athletes and to offset any educational disadvantages of athletic participation.

Today, advising student athletes seems to be a shared responsibility of athletic and academic departments (Mand and Fletcher 1986). Supportive advisers can help student athletes develop the thinking skills they need to solve problems and make decisions about academic planning. In collaboration with coaches, other members of the athletic staff, and faculty members, they can encourage student athletes to develop the kind of commitment to academics that they demonstrate toward athletics (Gurney and Johnston 1986; Kramer 1986a; Petitpas and Champagne 1988).

International students
In 1990, more than 386,000 international students attended college in the United States. The 5.6 percent increase over 1989 was the largest in seven years, and Asian students accounted for 9 percent of the growth (Wilson 1990). Most international students come from the Third World, more than half are undergraduates, and numbers of traditional-age freshmen are on the rise (Altbach 1989; Solomon and Young 1987; Wilson 1990). International students seem to place greater importance on academic and career goals than on nonacademic concerns. Although they generally make satisfactory progress toward academic goals, they cite lack of practical work experience and uncertainty about careers as areas of concern. Because the value systems of international students

are different from those of U.S. students, traditional student development theory might not apply to them (Bulthuis 1986; Cadieux and Wehrly 1986).

The time spent in U.S. colleges and universities can prove beneficial not only for international students, but also for U.S. students. Academic institutions are by nature international, with foreign students and scholars being "one of the most visible and important parts of the world-wide exchange of ideas" (Altbach 1989, p. 126). International students on U.S. campuses acquaint U.S. students with other cultures and often return to their countries with some of the norms and values of the United States. This phenomenon has important political, social, and economic implications (Altbach 1989). "Given the reality of global interdependence, the U.S. will gain significantly by strengthening its ties with students from other countries" (KaiKai 1989, p. 123).

Some concerns of international students are similar to those of U.S. students. Most college students are concerned about academic success, choosing the right college or university, choosing the right major, and developing good rapport with instructors and fellow students. But international students are also concerned about overcoming language difficulties and financial problems, adjusting to new cultural, social, and educational systems, and selecting relevant academic programs (Bulthuis 1986; Cadieux and Wehrly 1986).

The career and academic needs of international students seem to be greater than those of U.S. students in a number of important categories. International students express greater needs to obtain work experience in areas that interest them, explore job opportunities in their majors, develop effective job-seeking skills, and talk to counselors about career plans. They need to develop academic plans, including selecting courses and getting help from advisers. They also want to improve study habits and writing skills and to adjust to the expectations of U.S. instructors. Effective advisers of international students appear to focus less on developing study habits than on designing academic plans, especially those appropriate and relevant to international students' home countries (Leong and Sedlacek 1989).

The perceptions of non-Western international college students differ from those of Western students. For non-Western international students, instructors are not facilitators of learning but revered authorities. Generally, non-Western students

In some cases, advisers are the most important individuals international students encounter in the United States.

adhere to strict standards of excellence and see educational attainment as the primary way to achieve affluence and status. On the other hand, Western students are more likely to question instructors, display flexible attitudes toward academic excellence, and see educational attainment as only one way to achieve affluence and status. Advisers of non-Western international students might consider encouraging an open view about life-styles in the United States (KaiKai 1989).

Because international students are concerned primarily with achieving academic goals, advising is a critical part of their college experience. In some cases, advisers are the most important individuals international students encounter in the United States. Effective cross-cultural advising depends on attention to the way people think, feel, and act. Advisers could be called on to examine not only the attitudes, knowledge, and skills of students, but their own as well (Cadieux and Wehrly 1986).

The following advising activities can contribute to a relationship of shared responsibility between advisers and international students:

- *Develop rapport.* Become familiar with the cultural and academic background of international students and their reasons for studying in the United States. Show concern for them as individuals *and* as guests in this country.
- *Be prepared to explain many aspects of college.* International students might not understand the basic organization of U.S. institutions. Interpretation can contribute to the ongoing orientation that many international students need.
- *Become familiar with the student's level of preparation for college.* Determine which courses will challenge entering students without exposing them to situations for which they are inadequately prepared.
- *Recommend reasonable course loads at first.* Proficiency in English is critical to success in any course. Courses in English as a second language might be required.
- *Suggest practical work experiences.* Some international students return to positions of considerable responsibility in their home countries. They are concerned about the relevance of a U.S. education. Advisers can facilitate learning by suggesting internships, practicums, or other opportunities for professional experience.

- *Encourage involvement in college life.* Wide-ranging involvement in college activities can enrich the experiences of international students as well as those of the U.S. students with whom they interact. The resulting cross-cultural relationships can provide meaningful experiences.
- *Act as advocates.* Advisers can make other college constituents aware of the influence of international students on the community. Sometimes organized educational sessions help (Althen 1983; Cadieux and Wehrly 1986).

A shared advising relationship is particularly welcomed by international students. Advisers who assist international students as they reflect on their options, list possibilities, and make decisions can be effective translators of U.S. culture. They might find that their attitudes have influence beyond the immediate advising relationship and contribute to cross-cultural experiences on which future international relations can be built.

Students in Transition

All college students are in transition, but for some the transition process is more difficult than for others. Regardless of age or personal situation, some students are acutely aware of the process of integration into college life; others seem to adjust without effort. Perceptive academic advisers can help students make transitions if they encourage students to focus first on exploring life, career, and educational goals. Then students seem to be better equipped to select educational programs, choose courses, and schedule classes (Frost 1989a, 1989b; O'Banion 1972; Polson 1986; Tinto 1987).

While college is a time of change for all students, freshmen, students who are undecided about their majors or who change majors, transfer students, and adult students are students in transition of particular concern to advisers and advising coordinators. During transition, students make decisions that can profoundly affect the patterns of their lives. They seek support from advisers as they explore future directions. Advising can provide opportunities to introduce students in transition to a larger purpose of advising by sharing decision making with them as they adjust to college. Table 2 summarizes the characteristics of students in transition and recommended advising techniques for each group.

Academic Advising for Student Success

TABLE 2

STUDENTS IN TRANSITION: SUMMARY OF
CHARACTERISTICS AND TECHNIQUES FOR ADVISING

	Freshmen	Students with Undecided Majors
Characteristics Important to Advisers	• Stages of assimilation important • Must meet new expectations of peers and faculty • Academic integration influences development of academic skills • Social distractions negatively influence academic success • Negative reactions to college include irrelevancy, underpreparedness, uncertainty about majors and careers, incompatibility	• Heterogeneous population much like total student population • Many lack sense of identity • Many anxious about being undecided • Others need information only to decide on a major • Some need help with making decisions
Advising Techniques	• Consider students as individuals adjusting to a new environment • Be familiar with the stages of assimilation • Establish a supportive relationship early • Be attentive to fit between student and college • Emphasize academic success • Schedule regular contact at first, then increase student's responsibility	• Encourage students to discover interests and explore options before deciding about majors • Assure students that being undecided is acceptable, even desirable, for underclassmen • Maintain a positive attitude to change • Discuss specific decision-making techniques with students • Encourage students to be responsible to decisions

Transfer Students	Adult Students
• For most, process unlike that for freshmen	• Most have been away from formal education for at least two years
• Most have specific academic and career goals	• Most work full or part time
• Some have lower levels of attainment than nontransfers	• Education is usually not a primary concern
• Some miss the personal attention of community colleges	• Less involved with college life than traditional students
• Need to understand practical aspects of college	• Most manage multiple life roles
	• Bring life experiences to the classroom
	• Lack of time a problem
• View advising relationships as key to success	• View as developing individuals
• Display concern and interest, not just availability	• Understand adult stages of transition
• Orient students to college as well as advise them	• Understand students' reasons for enrolling
• Collaborate with sending or receiving institution	• Assist students in forming campus connections
• Analyze transfer credits as soon as possible	• Encourage academic planning
• Help students find the resources they need to remain in school	• Act as an advocate for adult students to provide equity for students

Advising freshmen: Orientation and beyond

Academic advisers are vital contributors to a new intellectual and social environment for freshmen. Sometimes the connection is a formal one; orientation and advising are integrated processes designed to enhance overall institutional fit. Other orientation programs are not formally connected to advising. In either case, advisers who enhance freshman students' success understand the process of becoming assimilated into college, the powerful influence of the campus environment, and advisers' roles in helping new students succeed in the academic community.

Students follow three stages of assimilation into college: (1) separation from communities of the past, (2) transition between high school and college, and (3) incorporation into the collegiate society (Tinto 1987). During separation, which most students find stressful to some degree, students dissociate themselves from their former communities of family, high school, and residence. Many readily accept the move toward adulthood, but some find the process so stressful that they leave college.

During transition, the following stage, students recognize that new norms and patterns of behavior define the college community. They base acceptance of the new environment on the degree of change they must undergo to become assimilated. Students from backgrounds having norms and behavior patterns very different from those of the college are likely to experience more stress than those from similar backgrounds. Financially disadvantaged students, underprepared students, first-generation college students, and other minorities are at risk during transition. Though external assistance can make a difference during separation and transition, the individual's willingness to become adjusted is essential:

> *The problems associated with separation and transition to college are conditions that, though stressful, need not in themselves lead to departure. It is the individual's response to those conditions that finally determines staying or leaving* (Tinto 1987, p. 98).

For most students, separation and transition occur early in the college experience. Then they adopt norms and patterns of behavior appropriate to the college setting. Most students, left to "make their own way through the maze of institutional life" (Tinto 1987, p. 98), depend largely on other members of the community for support. Some students make significant personal contacts on their own; others need formal structures to become involved in college.

In each year of college, academic integration appears to influence the development of academic skills. For freshmen and sophomores, academic integration seems to be the most important influence on the development of academic skills during those years. By the junior year, the influence of academic integration declines and social integration becomes more influential:

> *The potential academic benefits of helping new students become academically integrated may not be fully appreciated. Programs that introduce students to the intellectual world of college (e.g., orientation, academic advising by faculty members, freshman seminars, or other intellectual experiences tailored for freshmen) may play a critical role in students' subsequent levels of academic integration and, consequently, in their academic development* (Terenzini and Wright 1986, pp. 18–19).

Freshman advisers need not only to know how students achieve a good fit in college, but also to understand circumstances that can contribute to lack of fit, among them:

- *Academic boredom.* Freshmen placed in courses for which they are overprepared and students who experience poor teaching and advising often feel unchallenged. Of the 5,000 undergraduates surveyed in 1986 by the Carnegie Foundation for the Advancement of Teaching, 37 percent said they were bored in class (Levitz and Noel 1989).
- *Irrelevancy.* Students who do not feel that their college experiences are useful beyond the classroom often do not graduate. Nearly 40 percent of undergraduates consider general studies irrelevant to the subjects that interest them (Levitz and Noel 1989).
- *Limited or unrealistic expectations of college.* Students often have vague notions of what college is all about or enter with a wait-and-see attitude. Some come expecting to be dissatisfied. Others, especially first-generation college students, need a basic understanding of the structure of a college or university before they can participate in advising (Levitz and Noel 1989; National Institute of Education 1984).

- *Academic underpreparedness.* Many entering students lack basic skills and the will to seek assistance. They come to college expecting to fail or to perform above the predictions of entering scores and grades (Levitz and Noel 1989).
- *Difficulties in transition or adjustment.* Many freshmen do not feel welcome in college. About 40 percent of the respondents to the Carnegie Foundation's 1986 survey said that no professor at their institution expressed interest in their academic progress (Levitz and Noel 1989).
- *Lack of certainty about a major and/or a career.* This reason is the primary one given by high-ability students for dropping out of school (Levitz and Noel 1989). Those who are undecided about a major need to feel comfortable with their status.
- *Dissonance or incompatibility.* Many freshmen set themselves up for failure through their choice of curriculum, poor study habits, and other similar circumstances (Levitz and Noel 1989).

These findings have important implications for freshman advising. Some factors of the freshman year prove difficult for most students. The expectations of college professors are higher than those of high school teachers, course material is covered at faster rates, and students are expected to take more responsibility for their learning. Many freshmen must also adjust to new living environments, make new friends, and participate in new activities. They are in charge of their own time. Apportionment of time between classes, and for studying, social activities, and perhaps a part-time or full-time job is up to them. Freshmen experiencing low success identify their desires to achieve high grades, academic aptitude, and effort as factors most positively affecting their performance. Highly successful freshmen rate their desire to achieve high grades, academic aptitude, effort, *and* the ability to work hard and long on difficult tasks as important factors in success. Both groups identify social distractions as having a negative influence on success. While freshmen consider both academic and personal topics to be important, academic concerns are primary. Freshmen identify advisers as being among the most significant personal contacts they make and report that academic matters are the most significant they face. Therefore, freshman advisers should have an advantage. Both they and their area of concern appear to be important to freshmen

(DeBoer 1983; Okun et al. 1986; Pascarella and Terenzini 1978; Sagaria, Higginson, and White 1980; Terenzini and Pascarella 1980).

Freshman advisers not only help students remain in college, but also contribute to their success. Research suggests:

1. That faculty contact contributes to students' achievement, development of academic skills, involvement, and persistence (Astin 1977; Pascarella, Terenzini, and Wolfe 1986; Volkwein, King, and Terenzini 1986);
2. That early academic success, academic self-esteem, and effective study habits positively influence grades on final examinations (Overwalle 1989);
3. That freshmen rate as developmental those advisers who involve students in their college experiences, explore with students factors contributing to students' success, and show interest in students' academic and extracurricular progress (Frost 1990c);
4. That regularly scheduled contact between adviser and freshman appears to increase the developmental nature of the advising relationship and to heighten the student's satisfaction with advising (Chambliss and Fago 1987; Frost 1989b); and
5. That freshmen who become involved in their choice of curriculum seem to think carefully about their college careers (Frost 1989b).

Successful freshman advisers ask open-ended questions and encourage individual students to become involved in college. They usually take time to discuss strategies for study and managing time, and use of campus resources with their advisees, activities that seem to promote academic integration and positive freshman outcomes.

The environment and the organization of advising programs are other significant influences on freshmen. The influence of environment depends on at least three variables: site, demographics, and programs. If advisers understand the characteristics of students and where they came from (home, high school, and community) and the characteristics of the college, they are in positions to help students design academic plans that can to contribute to success during the freshman year. Such programs are attentive to fit; they represent an attempt to find a niche for each student (Banning 1989).

Successful freshman advising programs are not only important to students and to advisers, but are also essential parts of the collegiate organization (Levitz and Noel 1989). A number of institutions find it useful to integrate freshman orientation and advising into comprehensive programs for freshmen. Regardless of organizational structure, however, incoming students tend to view the two efforts as one. Students are unconcerned with administrative framework. What does concern them is whether or not their needs are being met in ways that contribute to their comfort and optimism about college.

Freshman programs with varying degrees of structure are offered by 78 percent of the 2,600 institutions surveyed by the American Council on Education, with smaller colleges reporting larger numbers of mandatory courses (El-Khawas 1984). Some are best described as orientation courses; others are full-fledged freshman seminars. While format varies, certain characteristics seem to be important. Most successful programs have the following attributes:

- *Concern for students as individuals.* The needs of individual students are considered.
- *Close interaction between faculty and new students.* Many institutions "front-load" freshman advising and orientation by choosing their best instructors to interact with freshmen in the classroom and in less formal settings.
- *Early emphasis on academics.* Freshmen report that they are most concerned with academic matters (Sagaria, Higginson, and White 1980). Studies and grades, selecting courses, and early exploration of majors and careers should be principal concerns of orientation and advising.
- *Small groups.* Students find small groups friendlier than large gatherings. Personal attention eases transitions. The use of small groups can begin in orientation and continue throughout the freshman year to provide academic information, social interaction, and personal support. In these groups, the stresses of transition can be discussed.
- *Attractive program materials.* As high school seniors, most students receive attractive recruiting publications. Materials for freshmen should be much the same—inviting and carefully prepared to avoid information overload.
- *Awareness of institutional resources.* Objectives include helping freshmen learn about available resources. Many

freshmen are unfamiliar with college bulletins and course syllabi. They might not be aware of instructional resources, student development services, and career counseling. If they are encouraged to learn about resources and become proactive about seeking the help they need, they soon become independent members of the college community (Chambliss 1989; Frost 1989a; Frost and Hoffmann 1986; Gordon 1989; Kramer and Washburn 1983).

Many freshman seminar courses are organized around these objectives.

[One goal is to] introduce the student to the nature and value of a liberal education. . . . [An] objective [of the freshman seminar] may be to establish closer ties between faculty and students while serving as a vehicle for faculty advising (Gordon 1989, pp. 192–93).

Regardless of structure, freshman programs that show concern for students as individuals, facilitate interaction with faculty in small groups, and emphasize academics and proactive use of college resources seem to enhance the developmental nature of advising, ease transitions, promote students' involvement in learning, and encourage persistence in college (Astone, Nuñez-Wormack, and Smodlaka 1989; Chambliss 1989; Frost 1989a, 1989b; Gardner 1986; Kramer and Washburn 1983; Kramer and White 1982).

Students with undecided majors

When all is said and done, the college should encourage each student to develop the capacity to judge wisely in matters of life and conduct. Time must be taken for exploring . . . and reflecting. . . . The goal is not to indoctrinate students, but to set them free in the world of ideas (Boyer 1987, p. 284).

Before or during orientation, most college students are asked to choose a major. While declaring a major is usually optional, many students perceive the label of "undecided student" as undesirable. Except for students with definite plans to enter fields that prescribe the curriculum from the first quarter of the freshman year, freshmen who are undecided about a major can have an advantage. Some who know they are undecided are more advanced developmentally than others who enter college with majors in mind and later change courses of study. If, as suggested, college is to encourage students *to develop the capacity* to judge wisely, then perhaps freshmen should defer selecting a major until later in their college careers.

Freshmen enter college at various stages of development. While those who are undecided might not differ significantly from each other in personal characteristics, they do seem to lack a clear sense of identity (Holland and Holland 1977) and are at varying levels of commitment to a choice of major or career. Indecisiveness has been linked to low achievement, lack of involvement, and attrition (Chase and Keene 1981; Peterson and McDonough 1985). Although indecision depends on a number of factors (Gordon 1982; Jones and Chenery 1980; Lucas and Epperson 1988), some characteristics seem to be typical:

- *Undecided students make up a large portion of the student population.* Some institutions encourage students to explore alternatives and welcome students who are not ready to declare a major. Undeclared students seem comfortable in this atmosphere and are likely to seek help in selecting a major. In institutions that urge all freshmen to declare a major, undecided students might be reluctant to identify themselves and remain underserved.
- *The group is a microcosm of the freshman class.* Undecided students are a heterogeneous population. Many have multiple interests and abilities to succeed in a variety of programs.
- *Many undecided students feel anxious about making educational or vocational choices.* For most, this anxiety is healthy and not debilitating.
- *Many undecided students know that they need concrete information before choosing a major,* and they are open to gathering information and exploring options.
- *Some undecided students need help in making decisions,* acquiring problem-solving skills before making satisfying and realistic decisions (Gordon 1985, pp. 117–18).

In general, undecided students fall into three categories: (1) entering freshmen who are unwilling, unable, or unready to commit to a major; (2) students who enter college with a declared major but change their minds during college; and (3) students who begin the junior year with no clear major or career choice in mind (Gordon 1984). Students in each category can benefit from specific academic advising practices and attitudes.

Entering freshmen make up the largest group of undecided students. They fall into three categories: those lacking information, those lacking appropriate decision-making skills, and those experiencing self-conflict. The first step in advising them is to identify students' specific areas of need (Carney 1975).

Freshmen lacking information might need only to assess their values, goals, and energy levels, might need information about academic offerings on campus, or might need to explore career options. By declaring their undecided status, these students admit a willingness to gather information before deciding. Open-ended discussions with the adviser and exposure to campus resources like department chairs, students majoring in their areas of interest, and the career planning office can be good beginning steps (Gordon 1984).

Other undecided freshmen might have sufficient information on which to base a decision but lack the decision-making skills to make a choice. Practice with small decisions is often a good way to begin. Advisers can encourage such students to develop a written four-year academic plan. The process of discovering alternatives and narrowing choices can prepare students for choosing a major (Frost 1989a; Gordon 1984).

The third subgroup of undecided entering freshmen seems to have personal or social concerns that preclude declaring a major. Their areas of interest might not align with their abilities or energy. Their choices might conflict with those of parents or other significant adults. Such students should first address the questions of who should decide the future and what criteria should be used. Then they can approach questions about a major (Gordon 1984). Students who perceive that being decided is preferred by the college need to become comfortable with their indecision and encouraged to explore alternatives. One essential factor seems to be a college environment that is open to exploring interests and options.

Students who change majors are the second category of undecided students. They make up 75 percent of the college population, attempt and pass more hours than students who do not change majors, have higher cumulative GPAs, and are

Some who know they are undecided are more advanced developmentally than others who enter college with majors in mind. . . .

more likely to persist to graduation than either decided or undecided students (Anderson, Creamer, and Cross 1989). Such students can benefit from understanding that, during transition to college, all initial choices of majors are tentative and that to explore alternatives is a healthy activity. Advising is most effective when students are ready to change majors but before they become discouraged and consider dropping out. Advisers who are accessible and maintain positive attitudes toward change can encourage students to rethink their goals, generate new alternatives, use credits already earned, understand the career choices available, and devise plans of action (Gordon 1984). Change of major can then become a developmental process in which students master new skills that are useful in other situations.

Intrusive advising might be necessary for two subgroups of undecided upperclass students: (1) those who have never made choices because they find it difficult to narrow options, are generally indecisive, or are immature; and (2) those who decide in the last two years of college to change majors. Advisers might encourage upperclass students who are considering several majors to eliminate some alternatives, set or reset goals, and see the advising process as a way to move toward achieving their goals. In extreme cases, these students need counseling beyond the advising relationship (Gordon 1984).

To be effective, advising programs for undecided students need administrative support. In organized programs, advisers help students explore their strengths and limitations. Advisers usually explain the career development process as it relates to differing stages of life and suggest ways for students to gather and consider information.

Advisers and advising coordinators who work in institutions dedicated to students' exploration, who are committed to developmental advising, and who blend career counseling with advising can help undecided students determine a major. As undecided students become comfortable with their indecisiveness, involve themselves in the advising *process,* ask open-ended questions, and seek answers from a variety of resources, they can make well-considered—and often permanent—decisions about majors and careers.

Transfer students
Students who transfer to other institutions after completing two-year college programs or who interrupt study at one insti-

tution and transfer to another undergo periods of transition unlike those of freshmen. Such students have survived the change from high school to college and need to learn to succeed in different, often larger, environments. They sometimes find it difficult to adjust to an environment that offers less personal attention from faculty and staff than that available at most two-year institutions. More than for some other groups, transfer students find it important to understand the practical value of higher education to future employment, which can affect their integration, performance, and satisfaction with the academic programs of receiving institutions (Johnson 1987).

The population of transfer students is a heterogeneous one, including a wide range of ages, races, and backgrounds (Harrison and Varcoe 1984). Researchers find it difficult to report numbers of students who transfer, but they do agree that the population is growing. In 1989, about 5.3 million students, or 43 percent of all undergraduates, were enrolled in community colleges. An estimated one-third of them transferred to four-year institutions (Watkins 1990). Transfer students usually have specific academic and career goals. They change majors less frequently and have a better sense of purpose than do freshmen. Their intellectual growth seems to be more influenced by the concern and interest of faculty than by frequent contact alone; therefore, advising relationships can be particularly important. Transfer students appreciate faculty who are interested in the growth of students inside and outside the classroom and view their contact with advisers as "a key ingredient in successfully capturing the knowledge to which they have been exposed" (Volkwein, King, and Terenzini 1986, p. 427).

It is surprising that transfer students receive little attention in discussions about retention. From the perspective of receiving institutions, transfers form a significant portion of the four-year college population. From one-fifth to one-third of the bachelor's degrees awarded go to students who began at another college (Volkwein, King, and Terenzini 1986). When considered from the perspective of the sending institution, the picture is less bright. Although one-third of community college students plan to attend four-year colleges, only one-fourth enroll; fewer actually receive bachelor's degrees (Watkins 1990).

Successful transfer is critical to minority populations. Two-year colleges enroll 43 percent of all African-American undergraduates, 55 percent of Hispanic undergraduates, and 57 percent of Native American undergraduates (Watkins 1990). To earn baccalaureate degrees, these students must find the process of transferring successful. While transfer seems to work for close to half of the students who experience it, minority students seem to be disproportionately represented in the half who could benefit from improvements. The two-year college students most likely to continue at four-year institutions have advantages in academic preparation and social skills. Minority students are underrepresented in this population ("Few Poor Students" 1990; Richardson and Bender 1987). Transfer students, especially African-American transfer students, exhibit significantly lower levels of educational attainment than do students who graduate from their initial college of enrollment (Kocher and Pascarella 1990). Their grades typically decline during the first term after transfer but improve in successive terms (Harrison and Varcoe 1984).

Programs designed to meet the needs of transfer students can benefit students in both the sending and receiving institutions, facilitate the process of transferring, and increase the likelihood that they will graduate from receiving institutions (Tinto 1987). Success can begin with four-year institutions' developing articulation programs with two-year institutions to encourage two-year college students to obtain appropriate information about the next level of college. Information about evaluating transcripts, advising, and registration can begin the transition process (Harrison and Varcoe 1984). Advising by receiving institutions should begin before transfer students leave the sending institution.

A Ford Foundation–supported effort to provide transfer opportunities to community college students provides an example of these suggestions. In 1983, Ford funded the Urban Community College/Transfer Opportunities Program (UCC/TOP). Because fewer African-American and Hispanic than white students transfer from community colleges to senior institutions, colleges with sizable minority enrollments were invited to participate in the program (Donovan and Schaier-Peleg 1988).

UCC/TOP recommends ongoing collaboration between two-year and four-year institutions. This interaction seems to be an important key to effective communication about transferring. Interinstitutional dialogue between administrators and faculty concerning curriculum, teaching strategies, and outcomes can close the communication gap for transfer students. UCC/TOP also recommends comprehensive data collection to track courses, grades, and credits. Computer systems that automatically detect students in academic difficulty and notify students and advisers about problems seem most helpful. Individual contact is also important. Researchers advise community colleges to appoint transfer counselors to work with academic advisers from both the sending and receiving institutions and initiate dialogue about students' academic programs between faculty at both institutions (Donovan and Schaier-Peleg 1988; Green 1988; Remley and Stripling 1983).

In general, transfer students view their contacts with academic advisers as key ingredients in successful transition to the receiving institution. Contact alone is not enough, however. Transfer students look to advisers at sending and receiving institutions to provide orientation and to ease the transition. Whether students transfer after completing courses of study at two-year institutions or interrupt their study at one institution to attend another, they need guidance in finding answers to questions about course credits, requirements for general education, and majors.

Providing academic orientation to transfer students at receiving institutions is unlike advising freshmen. Most freshmen learn about college in organized orientation programs; transfer students often discover resources and services on their own. Often advisers are a first contact on campus for transfer students and might be called on for orientation to support services, academic resources, and policies. Early in the advising relationship, advisers should suggest analyzing transfer credits to avoid misunderstanding at the time of graduation (Newhouse and McNamara 1982). Then advisers should consider encouraging transfer students to become involved in the receiving college community, especially the areas that emphasize the practical side of college.

Adults and other nontraditional students

"It has never been any secret that we change as we age. The only question is how" (Daloz 1986, p. 43). To respond to the question of how, change is linked to development. Development is defined not as change only, but as change with direction, change that is properly promoted by education (Daloz 1986). Because adults make up a significant college population and their numbers are increasing, advising coordinators and advisers of adults need to be familiar with trends in adult students, to recognize these students as individuals who are developing, and to understand adults' reasons for enrolling in college, the transitions they face as students, and how advisers can help them succeed.

At least 13.2 million college students are over age 25. This population, which represents 42 percent of all college students who earn credit, is 58 percent female, 63 percent married, 88 percent white, and 71 percent employed full time. By 2000, numbers of adults will be considerably larger; 75 percent of all U.S. workers will need to be retrained. They can be expected to continue to turn to higher education to develop skills and for personal fulfillment (Aslanian and Brickell 1988; Polson 1986).

Although some institutions use an age-related definition of adult students, a developmental definition seems more useful. Adult students are those who have been away from formal education for at least two years. Most work either full or part time and do not identify education as their primary concern in life. Decisions about persisting in college are more often affected by the external environment than by the variables of social integration that influence students of traditional age. While adult students have close relationships with faculty and become involved with peers and staff, they do not seem to become as involved as traditional-age students. Most are not active in campus social activities or concerns of the student body. Academic matters, problems of mobility, multiple life roles, integrating family, job, and college support systems, and developing a sense of belonging in the academic environment concern adult students. They also worry about how they relate to the traditional-age students in class (Bean and Metzner 1985; Polson 1986, 1989; Sloan and Wilmes 1989; Swift 1987).

Changing norms for women in the work force, rising standards of living, widespread acceptance of life-long learning, and increasing requirements for occupation-related learning during adulthood are factors that encourage adults to enroll in college (Cookson 1989). These trends indicate two sources of motivation for adult students: (1) pressures from the environment, such as changes in employment, family, or economic situations, and (2) pressures from the individual, such as changes linked to adult development or a search for satisfaction. But whether adults enroll because of personal preferences, employment requirements, or new career directions is not the central issue (Dean, Eriksen, and Lindamood 1987). While not all adult students are intrinsically motivated, most invite growth and seem willing to manage multiple roles while in school. The adviser's challenge is to help adult students find resources to assist in the integration of their existing roles with their new roles as students and to assist in planning educational programs that meet their short- and long-term needs.

Adults might feel out of the mainstream of college life and constrained by family and work from full participation in the academic program. As a group, they are committed to educational goals, yet isolation and incongruence can influence their decisions about staying in college. Adults usually attend college with a clear purpose in mind, want value for their money, have more commitments on their time than younger students, and bring varied and rich life experiences to the classroom and the advising relationship. They anticipate *and* perceive that job responsibilities, lack of time, not enjoying their studies, lack of confidence in their abilities, and the difficulties of course work are barriers to success. Job responsibilities seem to be more significant barriers than anticipated; lack of confidence in ability is anticipated to be a more significant barrier than experience indicates. Adult students report that the barrier most difficult to anticipate correctly is lack of time (Sloan and Wilmes 1989).

To be successful, adults could need intervention strategies that focus on the process of transition and on new ways to receive college services. Some institutions meet the needs of adult students more readily than others. By viewing adult students as marginal to the institution's overall mission, some colleges and universities limit services to them. In adapting to adult students, most institutions experience three stages of acceptance. During the first, or laissez-faire, stage, the system works neither for nor against adults. Barriers are removed, but positive intervention does not take place. The second stage is one of separation. Separate services, sometimes inferior to those for younger students, separate adults from the traditional-age student body. In the third, or equity, stage, adults receive the same quantity and quality of services as traditional-age students (Polson and Eriksen 1988).

Institutions overlooking the influence of the adult student population should consider that 60 percent of adult students seek a degree, 50 percent take four or more courses, and 25 percent study full time. Although services for nontraditional students seem directly related to administrative support, those services most accessible do not require major reorganization of the administration. Academic advising is one of them (Aslanian and Brickell 1988; Champagne 1987; Polson and Eriksen 1988; Richter-Antion 1986; Tinto 1987).

Effective advisers of adults recognize the stage of acceptance of their institution and, within this context, use developmental advising to address four distinct areas of concern: (1) issues of transition, such as fears regarding competency and adjustment to new roles; (2) a match between the institution's goals and the student's when they help students select courses and relate the purpose of prerequisites to the course of study; (3) the formation of campus connections; and (4) campus policies that are unfair to adults. Because most adults commute to class, advisers are often their only out-of-class contacts with college (Sloan and Wilmes 1989). Advisers not only give academic counsel but also often provide ongoing orientation and identify pathways to college services. In their roles as professionals in their fields, advisers also serve as role models for adults who enroll to enhance their careers.

Although many adults are "application" oriented and choose courses immediately applicable to their lives or jobs, effective advisers suggest that adults look at short- *and* long-term goals when determining a course of study. While they bring a wealth of experience to the advising relationship, adults are likely to take advice more seriously than do younger students (Bitterman 1985; Swift 1987). Advisers who treat adult students as adults and not as 18-year-olds, ask open-ended questions, and suggest campus or community resources that provide solutions to problems encourage adult students to become full participants in academic planning.

Advisers should also be aware of the stage of acceptance of their college or university and work to improve those attitudes and services most directly affecting adult students. By addressing the issues of how institutional rules and practices affect groups as well as individuals, advisers can promote equity for adults. Institutions concerned with removing barriers to the success of adults might consider training advisers in adult development theory, career development theory, and midlife career strategies (Polson 1986).

These discussions of student populations and their advising are reminders of the recommendation that advising not take place in isolation (Grites 1979). They concern advising at the student level. Concepts of developmental advising and academic planning have been considered in the context of students and advisers sharing responsibility for successful advising. Other tools for success at students' level are an understanding of the influence of advising on contacts between faculty and students, involvement, and persistence. The next section concerns advising at the institutional level. If colleges and universities have as a goal to plan and implement campuswide, student-centered systems of advising, certain attitudes and practices can contribute to success. Useful methods at the institutional level are much like those for students. They center around shared planning and focus on relationships that can contribute to positive outcomes for students.

SUCCESS IN ADVISING: Strategies for the Future

The first four sections of this monograph present tools for developing successful advising relationships, examining concepts of advising and populations for which they can be effective. But tools are not products. They are useful only as contributors to timely and effective advising services for students. Before advising programs can foster relationships of shared responsibility and encourage academic planning, they need institutional support. To this end, this section addresses institutional success in advising.

Empirical research suggests that most institutions are not satisfied with their methods of academic advising. Despite the work of researchers, authors, and practitioners, today's programs demonstrate little improvement over those of the last decade. Results of the 1987 ACT survey "depict a somewhat disappointing picture of the status of academic advising in American colleges and universities" (Habley and Crockett 1988, p. 74). Models that work on some campuses generally are not applicable to others—and for good reason. Students vary. Institutions vary. Although seven organizational models have been identified to assist administrators as they reorganize services and assess their strengths and weaknesses (Habley 1983, 1988b), reports of the assessment of successful programs are rare. Therefore, this volume proposes no specific models for advising. Rather, it investigates strategies for planning, implementing, and evaluating campus-specific programs.

Program Management: Move Forward with a Plan

Although scholars and practitioners recommend careful selection, training, and evaluation of advisers, these activities often seem to be neglected. Sixty-three percent of the institutions responding to the 1987 ACT survey have written policy and procedures statements for advising, yet only 29 percent train advisers and only 21 percent regularly evaluate the program's effectiveness. Nearly 45 percent of the respondents do not recognize or reward advisers for their service (Habley and Crockett 1988).

Selecting, training, evaluating, and recognizing advisers seem most useful when they are parts of a structured planning process. Today, many colleges and universities guide collective decision making through planning. One successful model is strategic planning,

> *. . . an analytical approach that encompasses an assessment of the future, the determination of desired goals in the context of the future, the development of alternative courses of action to achieve those goals, and the selection of courses of action from among those alternatives* (Uhl 1983, p. 2).

Determining direction, or formulating an idea of the future, is the essential first step in strategic planning. This direction then guides planners as they anticipate change and make decisions. Ideally, participants in planning consider the internal and external conditions that define the culture of the institution before they adopt specific actions. This consensus-oriented approach seems highly effective in college and university settings (Chaffee 1984; Cope 1981; Frost 1988; Keller 1983; Meredith, Cope, and Lenning 1987).

It seems that a structured mechanism for change, such as strategic planning, is warranted for advising programs. When asked to rate institutional effectiveness for eight goals of advising, respondents to the 1987 ACT survey most often chose the category "achievement somewhat satisfactory." The only goal rating "achievement satisfactory" concerned prescriptive advising, such as providing accurate information about policies, procedures, resources, and programs (Habley and Crockett 1988). Perhaps strategic planning, with its attention to mission and the environment, can provide a forum for participants to address questions about the effectiveness of advising and move forward to increase the positive outcomes of college.

A general mission of colleges and universities is to pursue scholarship and transfer knowledge to learners (Kramer 1985, p. 3). Within this framework, planners can investigate the contributions of academic advising to the mission of the college or university and define an institution-specific mission for advising. Questions about fundamental advising philosophy are appropriate. Should advising contribute to significant positive college outcomes for students? How is advising defined on the campus? What are the outcomes of advising on the campus? How can the definition of advising be changed to increase the likelihood of positive outcomes? If, as suggested, advising is a form of teaching (Crookston 1972), then these questions are not only appropriate, but also necessary. When posed as part of organized planning agendas, open-ended questions about the definitions and outcomes of advising can become parts of a strategic investigation of the future.

In 1986, the Council for the Advancement of Standards (CAS) published standards and guidelines for student services and development programs.

The primary purpose of an academic advising program is to assist students in the development of meaningful educational plans . . . compatible with their life goals. . . . Academic advising should be viewed as a continuous process of clarification and evaluation (p. 11).

This statement can serve as a beginning point for an advising mission that reflects an institution's general purpose and specific advising philosophy. Such a mission is most helpful when designed by representatives of all who participate in the advising process. Defining and adopting a mission are the first steps to collaborative planning for a new or revitalized advising program.

In the strategic process, planners develop goals after they adopt a mission statement. Strategically defined goals are specific plans that narrow the gap between what is and what should be (Cope 1981; Uhl 1983). Goals for advising should address specific needs; they should define a program dedicated to helping students move *from* clarifying objectives for life and career and developing educational plans *to* interpreting requirements and selecting courses (Council for the Advancement 1986). Other goals for advising include encouraging students to develop decision-making skills and introducing them to support services (Council for the Advancement 1986) (see table 3). The order of the Council's goals is important. Developing plans for life and career is *followed by* selecting courses and interpreting requirements. This order suggests a process of developmental advising. The opposite order could indicate a traditional, or prescriptive, approach.

Before defining specific objectives and action plans, a critical look at the advising environment is useful. Those colleges and universities engaging in institutionwide strategic planning might have external and internal scans that prove helpful. If such scans are not available, the process of gathering and analyzing information, opinions, and perceptions can contribute to planning. Some questions should be considered in the

Before defining specific objectives and action plans, a critical look at the advising environment is useful.

TABLE 3

MISSION STATEMENT FOR ACADEMIC ADVISING

The primary purpose of an academic advising program is to assist students in the development of meaningful educational plans . . . compatible with their life goals.

The institution must have a clearly written statement of philosophy pertaining to academic advising, which must include program goals and set forth expectations of advisers and advisees.

Academic advising should be viewed as a continuous process of clarification and evaluation.

The ultimate responsibility for making decisions about life goals and educational plans rests with the individual student. The academic adviser assists by helping to identify and assess alternatives and the consequences of decisions.

Institutional goals for academic advising may include:

- clarification of life and career goals;
- development of educational plans;
- selection of appropriate courses and other educational experiences;
- interpretation of institutional requirements;
- increasing student awareness of educational resources available;
- evaluation of student progress toward established goals;
- development of decision-making skills;
- referral to and use of other institutional and community support services, where appropriate; and
- collecting and distributing student data regarding student needs, preferences, and performance for use in institutional policy making.

Source: Council for the Advancement 1986, p. 11. Reprinted with permission.

scanning: How is advising perceived on campus? What student populations are served by the advising program? What populations need to be served? What are the advising needs of these students? What campus and community resources can help fill these needs? Do students learn decision making and problem solving in the curriculum? What changes does the institution face in the future? How will these changes affect advising at this institution? When considered in the context of mission and goals, answers to these questions can guide the detailed work of establishing or refining advising.

The next step is to define specific objectives. By this time, participants in planning have firsthand knowledge of opportunities, needs, and resources; they can begin to break new ground. Decisions about the format of advising, the selection, training, and recognition of advisers, and comprehensive evaluation should accompany discussions of more far-reaching issues. A few pertinent questions should be answered: How can students be motivated to participate in the process of advising? Do students possess decision-making skills that can be transferred to the advising setting, or will these skills have to be taught? What skills and attitudes should advisers possess? How can faculty and staff members possessing these skills and attitudes become partners in advising? How can they be cultivated in others? How will advisers be selected, trained, evaluated, and rewarded? How can advising become a collaborative, campuswide effort? How should the outcomes of advising be defined? How can they be evaluated? How can the results of evaluation be used to improve advising? When participants in planning address these questions, the advising *process* can begin to move in important directions. Planners who are committed to routine evaluation and proper use of data can project a dynamic and ongoing vision of advising at their institution.

Academic Advisers: Select and Train for Effectiveness
While students and their needs for advising are the principal concern of this monograph, students are just one-half of the advising picture: Advisers are the other. For advising to be a true *process,* the needs of both participants in the *relationship* should be considered. Successful advising depends on effective advisers, and advisers' effectiveness depends in part on how they are selected and trained for their responsibilities (Grites 1978).

The selection of advisers has been described as the cornerstone of a successful program, especially when advisers are selected on the basis of criteria for effectiveness and are not required to serve (Grites 1987; Wilder 1981). About half the respondents to the 1987 ACT survey use only instructional faculty in all departments to advise. Participation by choice is most likely in four-year public institutions; four-year private institutions are most likely to have criteria for selection of advisers. Sixty-eight percent of the respondents to the 1987 ACT survey have no criteria for selecting advisers. Most advisers are faculty members, but the number of professional advisers is increasing (Habley and Crockett 1988; King 1988).

Ideally, advisers are selected on the basis of criteria that reflect the goals of the program. Criteria for selection should address students' and the institution's needs and result from collaborative planning. Good advisers are interested in establishing caring relationships with students. They see students as growing, maturing individuals and are accessible to them (Crookston 1972; Ford and Ford 1989; Frost and Hoffmann 1986; Wilder 1981). When department heads, instructional faculty, noninstructional professionals, paraprofessionals, or peers with these attitudes are selected to advise, they can learn the skills they need in a variety of training formats.

A first step in training is to describe the responsibilities of advisers. While specific attitudes and practices are best defined by those familiar with the population of students and the institution, research-based guidelines are often helpful. Students seem to prefer the "personalized approach [that] is at the heart of developmental advising" (Gordon 1988, p. 113). They want advising relationships centered on academics and not on personal concerns, such as family matters or relationships with peers. They prefer advisers to supply information about such prescriptive items as requirements for graduation and course selection *and* to address broader developmental topics, such as exploring goals for life and career and planning a course of study (Fielstein 1989; Frost 1989b; Noble 1988; Winston and Sandor 1984).

Faculty members rated as developmental advisers by their students report that they address several areas of concern in their work with students, including personal attitudes and events related to college, such as classroom experiences, course content, and time management; group programs, policies, and opportunities, such as internships and opportunities for international exchange; and maintenance activities, such as signing forms, discussing procedures, and selecting courses (Frost 1990a, 1990c). Even though these findings highlight the importance of the concepts of developmental advising, most current training for advisers seems to center on prescriptive interactions (Habley and Crockett 1988).

Training advisers to address developmental advising and academic planning and to facilitate students' developmental needs includes attention to audience and content. Whatever the content, training is more successful when audience participation is high. It is important to include team-building activities and to recognize that some participants have extensive nonadvising duties (Barry 1989).

Several content questions are appropriate: What should advisers understand? What should advisers do? What should advisers know? (Keller 1988, pp. 156–57). Well-informed advisers understand the concepts of developmental advising, academic planning, and the development of higher education and of students that influence advising. The characteristics and needs of students, career planning, the relationship between advising and other student support services, and the responsibilities of advisers and advisees are also appropriate topics for discussion (Gordon 1984; Keller 1988). It is essential to explain academic regulations and procedures, especially to those who are advising for the first time.

Although most training occurs in workshops of one day or less, comprehensive preservice sessions followed by occasional in-service meetings are more effective. Other formats include workshops of more than one day, a series of meetings, and preservice training only. Although most advisers work individually with students, they seem to enjoy the periodic support and encouragement of their advising colleagues and interaction with those who support advising. Experienced and novice advisers can learn from each other, share enthusiasm for their responsibilities, and discuss mutual problems (Frost and Hoffmann 1986; Habley and Crockett 1988; Kapraun and Coldren 1982; Keller 1988).

Evaluation and Recognition: Essential Components
While evaluation should take place on many levels in well-executed advising programs, little research has been done to evaluate the effectiveness of academic advising. This situation is unfortunate because routine evaluation of advisers' training and performance can contribute to the program's overall effectiveness and allow success to be built on previous findings (Voorhees 1990). Evaluation used not for final judgments but to guide planning is usually considered most helpful. Then evaluators can become agents for change and point the way to improved advising services. They are sometimes the first to notice important trends in the student population (Brown 1978; Kramer 1990).

Evaluation indicates how well the advising system is working, documents the effectiveness of individual advisers for purposes of self-improvement, identifies areas of weakness to be addressed in future planning and training sessions, provides data for the recognition and reward of advisers, and gathers information to support requests for funding or other administrative contributions (Crockett 1988). When developmental advising enhances the decision-making skills of students and outcomes are measured, evaluation can be used to demonstrate positive educational outcomes for students (Frost 1989b, 1991).

Comprehensive evaluation includes feedback from advising administrators, students, and individual advisers. Thorough evaluators usually investigate all aspects of the program, using objectives identified in planning as criteria. Evaluators should address certain questions: Is the advising program contributing to the institution's mission? Does advising function according to the purpose and accepted definitions of developmental advising? Do students engage in academic planning with their advisers? Does the advising program meet the needs of all populations? Has advising adapted to changes in the institutional environment? Is a program to train advisers in place? Is it effective? Is evaluation ongoing and effective? Are advisers appropriately recognized and rewarded? Do students respond to the advising program positively? What are the outcomes of advising for students? How are these outcomes measured? How can the program be improved?

To aid in evaluation of advising, systematic evaluation of the overall student development program and each functional area is recommended to determine whether the educational goals and the needs of students are being met (Council for the Advancement 1986). Although methods vary, evaluators should use both quantitative and qualitative measures. Results should contribute to improvements in the program. A cross section of participants should plan and implement evaluation procedures. Results can then be analyzed, shared, and used to guide positive change. Broad-based collaboration and timely use of the results of evaluation can engender an advising *system* grounded in theory and shared responsibility that meets the changing needs of all participants and supports desired educational outcomes.

Although appropriate recognition of advisers is necessary if advising is to assume a place of greater importance in higher education, reward for advising is often neglected. Administrators and faculty identify reward systems as the category for change that is most likely to improve advising programs. Yet 44.4 percent of all respondents to the 1987 ACT survey have no such systems of recognition or reward (Habley and Crockett 1988; Kramer 1986b; Larsen and Brown 1983; Polson and Cashin 1981).

Most institutions that reward advising offer recognition in the form of minor promotions and consideration for tenure (Habley and Crockett 1988). Appropriate recognition can take many forms, including reduction of teaching load, committee work, or research responsibilities; salary increments; major or minor consideration in decisions affecting promotion and tenure; and awards for excellence. To be beneficial, recognition of advisers needs to become a planning issue, to address criteria of selection and effectiveness for advisers, and to reflect the importance the institution places on advising.

Collaboration: A Key to Excellence
To design or revise an advising program to include the components described in this section requires ongoing, collaborative effort. Advising spans many institutional boundaries and involves most students. Because the constituencies are diverse and numerous, change cannot be accomplished in a fragmented way. It must be planned. Even so, positive change cannot be accomplished in haste; evaluation should lead to improvements that define constructive change. While collaboration can take many forms, building connections among academic affairs, student affairs, and support services seems to be an important route to retaining students and encouraging success (Frost and Hoffmann 1986; Looney 1988).

In an example closely related to academic advising, the Urban Community College/Transfer Opportunities Program recommends that representatives from two-year and four-year institutions work together to improve transfer programs. UCC/TOP also recognizes the value of collaboration between two-year colleges and secondary schools. In such efforts, students receive the "benefits that can accrue from systematic collaboration" (Donovan and Schaier-Peleg 1988, p. 35).

The theme of collaboration also appears in the literature on advising. Recognized as a factor in retention on campus, advising is described as:

. . . *a campuswide responsibility [that] includes faculty advisors, professional counselors, student affairs professionals,*

*administration, admission recruiters, residence hall per-
sonnel, financial aid workers, librarians, clerical personnel,
and security officers. Retention is not the total goal of the
program, but the by-product of expanded services and
expanded teamwork . . .* (Glennen et al. 1989, p. 25).

Others describe advising programs in which collaboration
is central to success (see, e.g., Abrams and Jernigan 1984;
Trombley 1984). Considering the interactive relationship of
contact between faculty and students, and involvement and
persistence, it is not surprising that researchers advocate collaboration among educators. When college constituencies
work together, they serve as models for faculty-student and
student-student collaboration. As these interactions become
obvious, the likelihood of meaningful contact and students'
involvement in academic matters can increase. When academic advisers, advising coordinators and administrators, and
those who support advising efforts collaborate to offer an
advising program that is centered on developmental concepts
and focuses on students' needs, advising can become an
essential systematic enterprise of the institution.

Advising as a Systematic Enterprise

*Inherent in the model of institutional departure is the impor-
tant notion that colleges are in a very real sense* systematic
enterprises *comprised of a variety of linking interactive
parts, formal and informal, academic and social. Events
in one segment of the college necessarily and unavoidably
feed back and impact upon events in other parts of the institution. . . . To fully comprehend the longitudinal process of
departure, one must take note of the full range of individual experiences [that] occur in the formal and informal
domains of both the social and academic systems of the
institution* [emphasis added] (Tinto 1987, pp. 117–18).

This statement acknowledges the importance of people working together to achieve positive outcomes. For students, this
view describes an advising relationship based on shared
responsibility. For institutions, it defines an enterprise based
on collaboration. Educators are not the only scholars who
recognize the growing importance of collaboration. Futurist
authors in other fields use words like "involvement," "part-

nerships," "networking," "interdependence," and "synergy" when writing about innovations of the 1990s and beyond (see, e.g., Covey 1989; Kanter 1989; Naisbitt and Aburdene 1990). In this description of the next century, the power of the individual is apparent:

The first principle of the New Age movement is the doctrine of individual responsibility. . . . It is an ethical philosophy that elevates the individual to the global level. . . . Individual energy matters (Naisbitt and Aburdene 1990, pp. 298–99).

The value of systematic enterprises *and* the concept of individual responsibility can sharpen the views of those who work to improve the outcomes of college through advising. This monograph presents tools and methods for designing a system of advising. For maximum benefit, the system functions on two levels. On the institutional level, advisers, advising coordinators and administrators, and those who support advising cooperate to implement advising programs that employ a range of campus and community resources: Instructors, department chairs, career counselors, student development personnel, and professionals from the community are all vital contributors. For students, advisers and students function much the same way. Within their relationship of shared responsibility, they design, implement, evaluate, and refine academic plans for students.

An advising relationship focused in this way can do more than facilitate the selection of courses and registration. It can serve as a training ground for students' future behavior. As they progress through the curriculum, students solicit contacts once initiated by advisers. They handle decisions once guided by advisers. An advising relationship that is changing in the direction of greater responsibility by students can become a valuable life model for individual accountability.

The final section of this monograph presents recommendations and conclusions for improved advising, addressing the needs of students and of institutions. The theme of the summary is collaboration—as well as systems and individual responsibility.

An advising relationship . . . can become a valuable life-model for individual accountability.

RECOMMENDATIONS AND CONCLUSION

Academic advising is a means, not an end. When advising is based on shared responsibility and designed to help students discover meaningful academic plans, then courses and schedules become tools, not products of the advising relationship. Advising so defined can have a number of positive outcomes for students. In the process of designing plans, students can learn to frame appropriate questions, seek out needed information, and learn decision-making skills. Such programs offer advantages for institutions as well. They give students opportunities to engage in systematic academic planning and could enhance retention through students' involvement.

The following recommendations offer a beginning point for those who wish to consider an advising mission based on shared responsibility. The recommendations involve changes in attitudes as well as practices. They can be applied to large and small, public and private institutions. They are intended not as final solutions, but as a framework for planning. Following the recommendations are suggestions for administrators and advising coordinators, for individual advisers, and for academic and student services professionals who support advising. Like the recommendations, they are most effective when those who understand the college culture and its student populations adapt them for specific use.

Recommendations for Improved Advising

To implement an effective advising system:

1. *Consider advising as an institutionwide system centered around students' involvement and positive college outcomes.* Advising should serve the needs of all students and contribute to their success in college.
2. *Promote concepts of shared responsibility for both students and the institution.* This orientation can serve to involve students in their academic futures and to encourage positive outcomes of college.
3. *Begin the advising relationship with an awareness of the larger purpose of advising and move to an awareness of details.* This approach is important for students and for institutions. Advising should contribute to students' learning and success, not merely supply answers to specific questions. It should also contribute to the overall effectiveness of education.

4. *Plan for success.* All participants in advising should be involved in an ongoing, strategic effort to center advising around a meaningful mission. Individual students reflect this orientation when they engage in academic planning with advisers.

5. *Evaluate.* Evaluation of the overall program and individual contributors is an essential part of planning; results can provide direction for change.

6. *Collaborate.* Participation in a shared advising relationship leads students to contact many members of the college community for answers to questions that arise in academic planning. These resource persons then advise both formally and informally. Others support the process. Work to provide a collaborative model for students and encourage them to cooperate with their advisers.

To support these recommendations, the following suggestions are offered as agenda items for administrators and advising coordinators, for individual advisers, and for supporters of advising. Overlapping suggestions are not only unavoidable, but also desirable. All participants in advising can benefit from familiarity with all suggestions.

Suggestions for Administrators and Advising Coordinators
Successful advising programs have the support of the administration and are usually coordinated by a person who accepts responsibility for providing dynamic leadership to advisers and support personnel. The following suggestions are offered to administrators and coordinators who work as a team to accomplish an institutionwide system of advising.

1. *Plan the advising program carefully.* Keep the needs of the student population in mind and involve a comprehensive range of constituents in the planning process. When planning, (1) consider the mission of the institution and its particular advising goals; (2) be familiar with the external environment, especially research on students' involvement, contact between faculty and students, and persistence; and (3) know the populations being served, for they are the most important components of the internal environment. Students are individuals with individual needs. External and institutional research can guide plan-

ning for students from diverse backgrounds or students in transition.

2. *Use and teach developmental advising techniques.* When focused on positive educational outcomes, advising can become a valuable component of teaching.

3. *Be especially attentive to the needs of freshmen.* For freshmen, academic integration is the most important influence on the development of academic skills for that year (Terenzini and Wright 1986). A well-designed freshman advising program sets the stage for academic success throughout college.

4. *Before inviting advisers to serve, consider their strengths and levels of interest.* When advisers are carefully selected according to established criteria, they are more likely to be strong contributors to the program.

5. *Offer training for advisers routinely.* Include discussions about involvement, contact, persistence, and the characteristics of student populations. Find time for advisers to identify and explore their needs during training.

6. *Evaluate.* Program evaluation and evaluation of individual advisers are important strategies for a successful program. Results can be used to improve the program, provide information for planning, and demonstrate student outcomes.

7. *Recognize and reward advisers and others who contribute to the program.* Recognition of advisers is a valuable tool when used to increase ownership in and build support for the program.

8. *Consider advising as a dynamic process, not a finished product.* Use the results of evaluation continually to bring about positive change.

Suggestions for Individual Advisers

Advisers are critical contributors to any advising system. The following suggestions are directed to advisers who work to enhance their effectiveness.

1. *Consider the advising* relationship *as an opportunity to teach students.* Treat them as partners by sharing responsibility for advising with them.

2. *Become familiar with students as* individuals. Their skills and needs vary. Recognize those differences and stay informed about their progress.

3. *Begin the advising relationship with a discussion of the broader purposes of advising: to find a direction for the future and to help students create appropriate and dynamic educational plans.* Then move to questions concerning majors, courses, and schedules.
4. *Do not make decisions for students.* Encourage them to explore options, frame questions, gather information, and make decisions. Be conscious of moving to stages of greater responsibility for students as the relationship progresses.
5. *Encourage students to become involved with advising, with academics, and with nonacademic aspects of college life.*
6. *Collaborate to improve advising.* Willingness to cooperate with others provides a valuable model for students: (1) Participate in planning the advising program, as institutional experience and knowledge of the college culture make advisers valuable contributors to planning; (2) participate in training and learn about educational issues that influence advising and about the students served; (3) participate in evaluation of both the advising program and of individual performance. Encourage the use of results as a means of improvement. Be open to suggestions for positive change.

Suggestions for Supporters of Advising

As advising coordinators and individual advisers encourage students to talk to other members of the college community about their courses of study, those who support advising become contributors to the advising process. Department chairs, instructors, career counselors, personal counselors, and others have frequent and meaningful contact with students. The following suggestions are offered for these participants.

1. *Learn about the advising system and its many constituencies.* Participate in appropriate planning, training, and evaluation.
2. *Learn about techniques for developmental advising.* The concepts provide valuable tools for dealing with students in any setting.
3. *Be open to students' inquiries.* As students formulate academic plans, they seek the advice of many people. Adopt

a welcoming attitude and view encounters with students as opportunities to encourage them to plan.

4. *Work collaboratively with others to enhance the systematic approach to advising.* Collective efforts improve advising, and other campus efforts that contribute to students' success can also benefit.

Conclusion

The move from an advising program based on merely supplying answers to students' questions about scheduling and registration to a system of academic planning centered around shared responsibility will not take place in one term. Nor will it take place in one academic year. The move is a deliberate, collective effort that involves changes in practices *and* attitudes and requires considerable individual and institutional commitment.

A look at the historical development of advising suggests that change is difficult at best. While some answers to questions about broad-based approaches to advising exist, most programs still center on prescriptive activities. Even though research suggests that involved students are successful students, most advising programs do not seem to encourage students' involvement. They offer short-term relationships with advisers. If the current literature on advising has one theme, it is that of shared responsibility. This theme offers guidance for those who plan for and manage programs as well as for those who interact with students. It speaks to college and university administrators, to advising coordinators, to advisers, to those who support advising, and to students. If applied creatively and with an eye to the future, perhaps academic advising relationships can provide learning experiences that prove valuable to students during the college years and beyond.

REFERENCES

The Educational Resources Information Center (ERIC) Clearinghouse on Higher Education abstracts and indexes the current literature on higher education for inclusion in ERIC's data base and announcement in ERIC's monthly bibliographic journal, *Resources in Education* (RIE). Most of these publications are available through the ERIC Document Reproduction Service (EDRS). For publications cited in this bibliography that are available from EDRS, ordering number and price code are included. Readers who wish to order a publication should write to the ERIC Document Reproduction Service, 7420 Fullerton Rd., Suite 110, Springfield VA 22153-2852. (Phone orders with VISA or MasterCard are taken at 800-443-ERIC or 703-440-1400.) When ordering, please specify the document (ED) number. Documents are available as noted in microfiche (MF) and paper copy (PC). If you have the price code ready when you call EDRS, an exact price can be quoted. The last page of the latest issue of *Resources in Education* also has the current cost, listed by code.

Abrams, H.G., and L.P. Jernigan. 1984. "Academic High-Risk College Students." *American Educational Research Journal* 21(2): 261–74.

Allen, W.R. 1988. "Improving Black Student Access and Achievement in Higher Education." *Review of Higher Education* 11: 403–16.

Altbach, P.G. 1989. "The New Internationalism: Foreign Students and Scholars." *Studies in Higher Education* 14(2): 125-37.

Althen, G. 1983. *The Handbook of Foreign Student Advising.* Yarmouth, Me.: Intercultural Press.

American College Testing Program. 1984. "Athletes and Academics in the Freshman Year: A Study of Freshman Participation in Varsity Athletics." Research Report No. 151. Washington, D.C.: ACT Program and Educational Testing Service.

Anderson, B.C., D.G. Creamer, and L.H. Cross. 1989. "Undecided, Multiple Change, and Decided Students: How Different Are They?" *NACADA Journal* 9(1): 46–50.

Aslanian, C.B., and H.M. Brickell. 1988. *How Americans in Transition Study for College Credit.* New York: College Entrance Examination Board.

Astin, A.W. 1975. *Preventing Students from Dropping Out.* San Francisco: Jossey-Bass.

———. 1977. *Four Critical Years.* San Francisco: Jossey-Bass.

———. 1984. "Student Involvement: A Developmental Theory for Higher Education." *Journal of College Student Personnel* 25: 298–307.

———. 1985. *Achieving Educational Excellence.* San Francisco: Jossey-Bass.

Astin, A.W., H.S. Astin, K.C. Green, L. Kent, P. McNamara, and M.R. Williams. 1982. *Minorities in American Higher Education.* San Francisco: Jossey-Bass.

Astin, A., W. Korn, and K. Green. 1987. "Retaining and Satisfying Students." *Educational Record* 68(1): 36–42.

Astone, B., E. Nuñez-Wormack, and I. Smodlaka. 1989. "Intensive Academic Advisement: A Model for Retention." *College and University* 65(1): 31–43.

Backhus, D. 1989. "Centralized Intrusive Advising and Undergraduate Retention." *NACADA Journal* 9(1): 39–45.

Banning, J.H. 1989. "Impact of College Environments on Freshman Students." In *The Freshman Year Experience: Helping Students Survive and Succeed in College,* edited by M.L. Upcraft, J.N. Gardner, and Associates. San Francisco: Jossey-Bass.

Barry, M. 1989. "The Training of Teachers as Advisors." ED 312 789. 22 pp. MF–01; PC–01.

Beal, P.E., and L. Noel. 1980. *What Works in Student Retention: The Report of a Joint Project of the American College Testing Program and the National Center for Higher Education Management Systems.* Iowa City: American College Testing Program and National Center for Higher Education Management Systems. ED 197 635. 142 pp. MF–01; PC–06.

Bean, J.P. 1985. "Interaction Effects Based on Class Level in an Explanatory Model of College Student Dropout Syndrome." *American Educational Research Journal* 22(1): 35–64.

Bean, J.P., and B.S. Metzner. 1985. "A Conceptual Model of Nontraditional Undergraduate Student Attrition." *Review of Educational Research* 55(4): 485–540.

Beasley-Fielstein, L. 1986. "Student Perceptions of the Developmental Adviser-Advisee Relationship." *NACADA Journal* 6(2): 107–17.

Biggs, D.A., J.S. Brodie, and W.J. Barnhart. 1975. "The Dynamics of Undergraduate Academic Advising." *Research in Higher Education* 3: 345–57.

Bitterman, J.E. 1985. "Academic Advising and Adult Education: An Emerging Synthesis." *NACADA Journal* 5(2): 29–33.

Blann, F.W. 1985. "Intercollegiate Athletic Competition and Students' Educational and Career Plans." *Journal of College Student Personnel* 26: 115–18.

Bohn, M.J., Jr. 1973. "Personality Variables in Successful Work-Study Performance." *Journal of College Student Personnel* 14: 135–40.

Borgard, J.H. 1981. "Toward a Pragmatic Philosophy of Academic Advising." *NACADA Journal* 1(1): 1–6.

Borgard, J.H., P.A. Hornbuckle, and J. Mahoney. 1977. "Faculty Perceptions of Academic Advising." *NASPA Journal* 14(3): 4–10.

Boyer, E.L. 1987. *College: The Undergraduate Experience in America.* New York: Harper & Row.

Brown, R.D. 1978. "How Evaluation Can Make a Difference." In *Evaluating Program Effectiveness,* edited by G. Hanson. New Directions for Student Services No. 1. San Francisco: Jossey-Bass.

Bulthuis, J.D. 1986. "The Foreign Student Today: A Profile." In *Guiding the Development of Foreign Students,* edited by K.R. Pyle. San

Francisco: Jossey-Bass.

Cadieux, R.A.J., and B. Wehrly. 1986. "Advising and Counseling the International Student." In *Guiding the Development of Foreign Students,* edited by K.R. Pyle. San Francisco: Jossey-Bass.

Carberry, J.D., M. Baker, and D.L. Prescott. 1986. "Applying Cognitive Development Theory in the Advising Setting." *NACADA Journal* 6(2): 13–18.

"Carnegie Survey of Undergraduates." 5 February 1986. *Chronicle of Higher Education:* 27–30.

Carney, C. 1975. "Psychological Dimensions of Career Development: An Overview and Application." Paper presented at a training conference for the Ohio Department of Education, April, Columbus, Ohio.

Carstensen, D., and C. Silberhorn. 1979. "A National Survey of Academic Advising: Final Report." Iowa City: American College Testing Program. ED 232 525. 15 pp. MF–01; PC–01.

Cesa, Thomas L. 1979. "Undergraduate Leavers and Persisters at Berkeley: Results of a Telephone Survey Conducted in Spring 1979." Paper based on a speech presented at an annual conference of the California Association of Institutional Research. ED 187 294. 55 pp. MF–01; PC–03.

Chaffee, E.E. 1984. "Successful Strategic Management in Small Private Colleges." *Journal of Higher Education* 55: 212–41.

Chambliss, C. 1989. "Comprehensive Freshman Advising." ED 304 968. 13 pp. MF–01; PC–01.

Chambliss, C.A., and G. Fago. 1987. "The Ursinus College Freshman Advising Program." *NACADA Journal* 7(2): 20–22.

Champagne, D.E. 1987. "Planning Developmental Interventions for Adult Students." Paper presented at an annual meeting of the American College Personnel Association/National Association of Student Personnel Administrators, March, Chicago, Illinois. ED 279 916. 22 pp. MF–01; PC–01.

Chase, C.I., and J.M. Keene. 1981. "Major Declaration and Academic Motivation." *Journal of College Student Personnel* 22: 496–502.

Chickering, A.W. 1969. *Education and Identity.* San Francisco: Jossey-Bass.

Chickering, A.W., and Z.F. Gamson. 1987. "Seven Principles for Good Practice in Undergraduate Education." *AAHE Bulletin* 39(7): 3–7.

Cibik, M.A., and S.L. Chambers. 1991. "Similarities and Differences among Native Americans, Hispanics, Blacks, and Anglos." *NASPA Journal* 28(2): 129–39.

Cookson, P.S. 1989. "Recruiting and Retaining Adult Students: A Practice Perspective." In *Recruiting and Retaining Adult Students,* edited by P.S. Cookson. New Directions for Continuing Education No. 41. San Francisco: Jossey-Bass.

Cope, R.G. 1981. *Strategic Planning, Management, and Decision Making.* AAHE-ERIC Higher Education Research Report No. 9.

Washington, D.C.: American Association for Higher Education. ED 217 825. 75 pp. MF–01; PC–03.

Council for the Advancement of Standards (CAS). 1986. *Standards and Guidelines for Student Services/Development Programs.* Iowa City: American College Testing Program.

Covey, S.R. 1989. *The Seven Habits of Highly Effective People: Restoring the Character Ethic.* New York: Simon & Schuster.

Crockett, D.S. 1982. "Academic Advising Delivery Systems." In *Developmental Approaches to Academic Advising,* edited by R.B. Winston, Jr., S.C. Ender, and T.K. Miller. New Directions for Student Services No. 17. San Francisco: Jossey-Bass.

———. 1988. "Evaluating and Rewarding Advisors." In *The Status and Future of Academic Advising: Problems and Promise,* edited by W.R. Habley. Iowa City: American College Testing Program.

Crockett, D.S., and R.S. Levitz. 1983. *A National Survey of Academic Advising.* ACT National Center for the Advancement of Educational Practices.

Crookston, B.B. 1972. "A Developmental View of Academic Advising as Teaching." *Journal of College Student Personnel* 13: 12–17.

Crosson, P.H. 1988. "Four-Year College and University Environments for Minority Degree Achievement." *Review of Higher Education* 11: 365–82.

Daloz, L.A. 1986. *Effective Teaching and Mentoring: Realizing the Transformational Power of Adult Learning Experiences.* San Francisco: Jossey-Bass.

Dassance, C.R., and R.L. Batdorf. 1980. "Educational Advising for Retention: Applying the Student Development Model." Forum presented at an annual convention of the American Association of Community and Junior Colleges, March, San Francisco, California. ED 190 176. 25 pp. MF–01; PC–01.

Dean, G.J., J.P. Eriksen, and S.A. Lindamood. 1987. "Adults in Midcareer Change: Case Studies for Advisors." *NACADA Journal* 7(2): 16–26.

DeBoer, G.E. 1983. "The Importance of Freshman Students' Perceptions of the Factors Responsible for First-term Academic Performance." *Journal of College Student Personnel* 24: 344–49.

Donovan, R. 1984. "Path Analysis of a Theoretical Model of Persistence in Higher Education among Low-income Black Youth." *Research in Higher Education* 21: 243–52.

Donovan, R., and B. Schaier-Peleg. 1988. "Making Transfer Work." *Change* 20(1): 33–37.

Downing, F. Spring 1981. "The National Academic Advisors' Association: An Historical Perspective." *National Adviser:* 3–8.

Earl, W.R. 1988. "Intrusive Advising of Freshmen in Academic Difficulty." *NACADA Journal* 8(2): 27–33.

Eddins, D.D. 1982. "A Causal Model of the Attrition of Specially Admitted Black Students in Higher Education." Paper presented at an annual meeting of the American Educational Research Association, March, New York, New York. ED 224 422. 55 pp. MF–01; PC–03.

El-Khawas, E. 1984. "Campus Trends." Higher Education Panel. Washington, D.C: American Council on Education. ED 252 171. 29 pp. MF–01; PC–02.

Ender, S.C. 1983. "Assisting High Academic Risk Athletes: Recommendations for the Academic Advisor." *NACADA Journal* 3(2): 1–10.

Ender, S.C., R.B. Winston, and T.K. Miller. 1982. "Academic Advising as Student Development." In *Developmental Approaches to Academic Advising,* edited by R.B. Winston, Jr., S.C. Ender, and T.K. Miller. New Directions for Student Services No. 17. San Francisco: Jossey-Bass.

Ervin, L., S.A. Saunders, H.L. Gillis, and M.C. Hogrebe. 1985. "Academic Performance of Student Athletes in Revenue-Producing Sports." *Journal of College Student Personnel* 26: 119–23.

Estrada, L.F. 1988. "Anticipating the Demographic Future: Dramatic Changes Are on the Way." *Change* 20(3): 14–19.

"Few Poor Students Found to Move from 2-Year to 4-Year Institutions." 17 January 1990. *Chronicle of Higher Education:* A35.

Fielstein, L.L. 1987. "Student Preferences for Personal Contact in a Student-Faculty Advising Relationship." *NACADA Journal* 7(2): 34–40.

———. 1989. "Student Priorities for Academic Advising: Do They Want a Personal Relationship?" *NACADA Journal* 9(1): 33–38.

Fiske, E.B. 1988. "The Undergraduate Hispanic Experience: A Case of Juggling Two Cultures." *Change* 20(3): 29–33.

Flannelly, S.J., and T.R. Sanford. 1990. "Student/Faculty Contact and Academic Quality of Effort: Excerpted Results from CSEQ Surveys, 1985–1989." Paper presented at an annual conference of the Southern Association for Institutional Research, October, Fort Lauderdale, Florida. ED 323 869. 5 pp. MF–01; PC–01.

Fleming, J. 1984. *Blacks in College.* San Francisco: Jossey-Bass.

Fonosch, G.G., and L.O. Schwab. 1981. "Attitudes of Selected University Faculty Members toward Disabled Students." *Journal of College Student Personnel* 5: 229–35.

Ford, J. 1983. "Producing a Comprehensive Academic Advising Handbook." *NACADA Journal* 2(1): 61–68.

Ford, J., and S.S. Ford. 1989. "A Caring Attitude and Academic Advising." *NACADA Journal* 9(2): 43–46.

Frost, S.H. 1988. *Strategic Academic Management: Innovation in Planning.* Athens: Univ. of Georgia. HE 024 087. 38 pp. MF–01; PC–02.

———. 1989a. "Academic Responsibility: Can It Be Taught?" *NACADA Journal* 9(2): 17–24.

———. 1989b. "The Effects of Academic Advising and the Frequency of Faculty Contact on the Cognitive Development of College Freshmen." Ed.D. dissertation, Univ. of Georgia.

———. 1990a. "Academic Advising for College and Beyond." HE 024 295. 7 pp. MF–01; PC–01.

———. 1990b. "A Comparison of Developmental Advising at Two Small Colleges." *NACADA Journal* 10(2): 9–13.

———. 1990c. "Educational Improvement through Academic Advising: Advisor Attitudes and Practices that Make a Difference." Paper presented at an annual conference of the Southern Association for Institutional Research, October, Fort Lauderdale, Florida. HE 024 089. 15 pp. MF–01; PC–01.

———. 1991. "Fostering the Critical Thinking of College Women through Academic Advising and Faculty Contact." *Journal of College Student Development* 32: 359–66.

Frost, S.H., and S.L. Hoffmann. 1986. *Act I: The Freshman Year Experience.* HE 023 412. 11 pp. MF–01; PC–01.

———. 1988. "Networking Partnerships: The Act I Program at Brenau College." *Proceedings: The 1988 East Conference of the Freshman Year Experience:* 58.

Gardner, J.N. 1986. "The Freshman Year Experience." *College and University* 61(4): 261–74.

Gish, D.L., and D.J. Dentler. 1989. "Life Planning: Enabling Comprehensive Advising at Small Institutions." *NACADA Journal* 9(1): 81–83.

Glennen, R.E., and D.M. Baxley. 1985. "Reduction of Attrition through Intrusive Advising." *NASPA Journal* 22(3): 10–14.

Glennen, R.E., P.J. Farren, F. Vowell, and L. Black. 1989. "Expanding the Advising Team." *NACADA Journal* 9(2): 25–30.

Gordon, V.N. 1982. "Reasons for Entering College and Academic and Vocational Preferences." *Journal of College Student Personnel* 23(5): 371–77.

———. 1984. *The Undecided College Student.* Chicago: Charles C. Thomas.

———. 1985. "Students with Uncertain Academic Goals." In *Increasing Student Retention,* edited by L.Noel, R. Levitz, D. Saluri, and Associates. San Francisco: Jossey-Bass.

———. 1988. "Developmental Advising." In *The Status and Future of Academic Advising: Problems and Promise,* edited by W.R. Habley. Iowa City: American College Testing Program.

———. 1989. "Origins and Purposes of the Freshman Seminar." In *The Freshman Year Experience: Helping Students Survive and Succeed in College,* edited by M.L. Upcraft, J.N. Gardner, and Associates. San Francisco: Jossey-Bass.

Gordon, V.N., R.W. Swenson, L. Spencer, D.I. Kline, M. Bogenschutz, and B. Seeger. 1988. "Advising as a Profession." *NACADA Journal* 8(2): 59–64.

Green, D.W. 1988. "Are Transfer Students Second Rate?" *College and*

University 63(3): 248–55.

Green, M.F. 1989. *Minorities on Campus: A Handbook for Enhancing Diversity.* Washington, D.C.: American Council on Education.

Grites, T.J. 1978. "Maximizing the Use of Faculty Advisors." ED 247 820. 16 pp. MF–01; PC–01.

———. 1979. *Academic Advising: Getting Us through the Eighties.* AAHE-ERIC Higher Education Research Report No. 7. Washington, D.C.: American Association for Higher Education. ED 178 023. 74 pp. MF–01; PC–03.

———. 1982. "Advising for Special Populations." In *Developmental Approaches to Academic Advising,* edited by R.B. Winston, Jr., S.C. Ender, and T.K. Miller. New Directions for Student Services No. 17. San Francisco: Jossey-Bass.

———. 1987. "Student Development through Academic Advising: A 4×4 Model." *NASPA Journal* 14(3): 35–37.

Gurney, G.S., and S.P. Johnston. 1986. "Advising the Student-Athlete." *NACADA Journal* 6(1): 27–29.

Gurney, G.S., and D.L. Stuart. 1987. "Effects of Special Admission, Varsity Competition, and Sports on Freshman Student-Athletes' Academic Performance." *Journal of College Student Personnel* 28(4): 298–302.

Habley, W.R. 1981. "Academic Advisement: The Critical Link in Student Retention." *NASPA Journal* 18(4): 45–50.

———. 1983. "Organizational Structures for Academic Advising: Models and Implications." *Journal of College Student Personnel* 24(6): 535–40.

———. 1988a. "Introduction and Overview." In *The Status and Future of Academic Advising: Problems and Promise,* edited by W.R. Habley. Iowa City: American College Testing Program.

———. 1988b. "The Organization of Advising Services." In *The Status and Future of Academic Advising: Problems and Promise,* edited by W.R. Habley. Iowa City: American College Testing Program.

———, ed. 1988c. *The Status and Future of Academic Advising: Problems and Promise.* Iowa City: American College Testing Program.

Habley, W.R., and D.S. Crockett. 1988. "The Third ACT National Survey of Academic Advising." In *The Status and Future of Academic Advising: Problems and Promise,* edited by W.R. Habley. Iowa City: American College Testing Program.

Hameister, B.G. 1989. "Disabled Students." In *The Freshman Year Experience: Helping Students Survive and Succeed in College,* edited by M.L. Upcraft, J.N. Gardner, and Associates. San Francisco: Jossey-Bass.

Hardin, C.J. 1988. "Access to Higher Education: Who Belongs?" *Journal of Developmental Education* 12(1): 2–19.

Harrison, C.H., and K. Varcoe. 1984. "Orienting Transfer Students." In *Orienting Students to College,* edited by M.L. Upcraft. San Francisco: Jossey-Bass.

Hines, E.R. 1981. "Academic Advising: More Than a Placebo?" *NAC-ADA Journal* 1(2): 24–28.

"Hispanic Students Continue to Be Distinctive." 1988. Change Trend-lines. *Change* 20(3): 43–47.

Holland, J.L., and J.E. Holland. 1977. "Vocational Indecision: More Evidence and Speculation." *Journal of Counseling Psychology* 24: 404–14.

Hughes, M.S. 1987. "Black Students' Participation in Higher Education." *Journal of College Student Personnel* 28: 533–45.

Isakson, R.L., J.M. Lawson, and J.D. MacArthur. 1987. "Student Development and the College Curriculum: What Is the Connection?" *NASPA Journal* 25(1): 70–78.

Ivory, S.T. 1986. "Campuses Expand Services for Disabled Students." *Higher Education and National Affairs* 35(17): 1+.

Janasiewicz, B.A. 1987. "Campus Leaving Behavior." *NACADA Journal* 7(2): 23–30.

Johnson, N.T. 1987. "Academic Factors That Affect Transfer Student Persistence." *Journal of College Student Personnel* 28: 323–29.

Jones, L.K., and M.F. Chenery. 1980. "Multiple Subtypes among Vocationally Undecided College Students: A Model and Assessment Instrument." *Journal of Counseling Psychology* 27(5): 469–77.

KaiKai, S.M. 1989. "Accommodating Diversity." *College Teaching* 37(4): 123–25.

Kalivoda, K.S., and J.L. Higbee. 1989. "Students with Disabilities in Higher Education: Redefining Access." *Journal of Educational Opportunity* 4(1): 14–21.

Kalivoda, K.S., F.S. Young, and D.L. Wahlers. 1989. *Students with Disabilities: A Guide for Faculty and Staff.* Athens: Univ. of Georgia. HE 024 086. 26 pp. MF–01; PC–02.

Kanter, R.M. 1989. *When Giants Learn to Dance: Mastering the Challenges of Strategy, Management, and Careers in the 1990s.* New York: Simon & Schuster.

Kapraun, E.D, and D.W. Coldren. 1982. "Academic Advising to Facilitate Student Retention." *NACADA Journal* 2(2): 59–69.

Keller, G. 1983. *Academic Strategy: The Management Revolution in Higher Education.* Baltimore: Johns Hopkins Univ. Press.

Keller, M. 1988. "Advisor Training." In *The Status and Future of Academic Advising: Problems and Promise,* edited by W.R. Habley. Iowa City: American College Testing Program.

King, M.C. 1988. "Advising Delivery Systems." In *The Status and Future of Academic Advising: Problems and Promise,* edited by W.R. Habley. Iowa City: American College Testing Program.

Kocher, E., and E. Pascarella. 1990. "The Impact of Four-Year College Transfer on the Early Status Attainment of Black-American and White-American Students." *Journal of College Student Development* 31: 169–75.

Kohlberg, L., and R. Mayer. 1979. "Development as the Aim of Education." In *Adolescent's Development and Education: A Janus Knot*, edited by R.H. Mosher. Berkeley, Cal.: McCutchan Publishing Corp.

Kozloff, J. 1985. "Delivering Academic Advising: Who, What, and How?" *NACADA Journal* 5(2): 69-75.

Kramer, G.L. 1990. "The Compleat Advisor: President's Address Delivered at the 1989 NACADA Conference, Houston, TX." *NACADA Journal* 10(1): 5-7.

Kramer, G.L., and R.W. Spencer. 1989. "Academic Advising." In *The Freshman Year Experience: Helping Students Survive and Succeed in College,* edited by M.L. Upcraft, J.N. Gardner, and Associates. San Francisco: Jossey-Bass.

Kramer, G.L., L. Taylor, B. Chynoweth, and J. Jensen. 1987. "Developmental Academic Advising: A Taxonomy of Services." *NASPA Journal* 24(4): 23-31.

Kramer, G.L., and R. Washburn. 1983. "The Perceived Orientation Needs of New Students." *Journal of College Student Personnel* 24: 311-19.

Kramer, G.L., and M.T. White. 1982. "Developing a Faculty Mentoring Program: An Experiment." *NACADA Journal* 2(2): 47-58.

Kramer, H.C. 1985. "Advising: Supporting the Academy." Position Paper. ED 272 062. 23 pp. MF-01; PC-01.

———. 1986a. "Faculty Advising: Help for Student-Athletes?" *NACADA Journal* 6(1): 67-79.

———. 1986b. "Faculty Development: The Advising Coordinator's Changing Scene." *NACADA Journal* 6(2): 31-42.

Kriegsman, K.H., and D.B. Hershenson. 1987. "A Comparison of Able-Bodied and Disabled College Students of Erikson's Ego Stages and Maslow's Needs Levels." *Journal of College Student Personnel* 28: 48-53.

Larsen, M.D., and B.M. Brown. 1983. "Rewards for Academic Advising: An Evaluation." *NACADA Journal* 3(2): 53-60.

Leong, F.T.L., and W.E. Sedlacek. 1989. "Academic and Career Needs of International and United States College Students." *Journal of College Student Development* 30: 106-11.

Levitz, R., and L. Noel. 1989. "Connecting Students to Institutions: Key to Retention and Success." In *The Freshman Year Experience: Helping Students Survive and Succeed in College,* edited by M.L. Upcraft, J.N. Gardner, and Associates. San Francisco: Jossey-Bass.

Looney, S.C. 1988. "Concerning Changes in Advising." In *The Status and Future of Academic Advising: Problems and Promise,* edited by W.R. Habley. Iowa City: American College Testing Program.

Lucas, M., and D. Epperson. 1988. "Personality Types in Vocationally Undecided Students." *Journal of College Student Development* 29: 460-67.

Lyons, A.W. 1985. "Applying Humanistic and Behavioral Principles to Assist High-Risk Freshmen." Research Report. ED 252 692. 10

---

pp. MF–01; PC–01.

McCauley, D.P. 1988. "Effects of Specific Factors on Blacks' Persistence at a Predominantly White University." *Journal of College Student Development* 29: 49–51.

McGuire, J.M., and J.M. O'Donnell. 1989. "Helping Learning-Disabled Students to Achieve." *College Teaching* 37(1): 29–32.

McLaughlin, B. 1986. "Advising College Athletes in the 1980s: A Higher Education Abstracts Review." *NACADA Journal* 6(1): 31–38.

McLaughlin, B.M., and E.A. Starr. 1982. "Academic Advising Literature since 1965: A *College Student Personnel* Abstracts Review." *NACADA Journal* 2(2): 14–23.

McPhee, S. 1990. "Addressing the Attrition of Minority Students on Predominantly White Campuses: A Pilot Study." *College Student Affairs Journal* 10(1): 15–22.

McQuilkin, J.I., C.B. Freitag, and J.L. Harris. 1990. "Attitudes of College Students toward Handicapped Persons." *Journal of College Student Development* 31: 17–22.

Mahoney F.A. 1982. "Guidance and Planning with Diversely Prepared Students." In *Diverse Student Populations: Benefits and Issues,* edited by Clark Taylor. New Directions for Experiential Learning No. 17. San Francisco: Jossey-Bass.

Mallinckrodt, B. 1988. "Student Retention, Social Support, and Dropout Intention: Comparison of Black and White Students." *Journal of College Student Development* 29: 61–64.

Mand, B., and H.J. Fletcher. Fall 1986. "The NAAAA: 10 Years Old and Changing." *Academic Athletic Journal:* 1–14.

Marion, P.B., and E.V. Iovacchini. 1983. "Services for Handicapped Students in Higher Education: An Analysis of National Trends." *Journal of College Student Development* 24: 131–39.

Mash, D.J. 1978. "Academic Advising: Too Often Taken for Granted." *College Board Review* 107: 33–36.

Meredith, M., R.G. Cope, and O.T. Lenning. 1987. *Differentiating Bona Fide Strategic Planning from Other Planning.* ED 287 329. 63 pp. MF–01; PC–03.

Miller, T.K., and S. McCaffrey. 1982. "Student Development Theory: Foundations for Academic Advising." In *Developmental Approaches to Academic Advising,* edited by R.B. Winston, Jr., S.C. Ender, and T.K. Miller. New Directions for Student Services No. 17. San Francisco: Jossey-Bass.

"Minority Access: A Question of Equity." 1987. Change Trendlines. *Change* 19(3): 35–43.

Moore, K.M. 1976. "Faculty Advising: Panacea or Placebo?" *Journal of College Student Personnel* 17: 371–75.

Naisbitt, J., and P. Aburdene. 1990. *Megatrends 2000: Ten New Directions for the 1990s.* New York: William Morrow & Co.

National Institute of Education. 1984. *Involvement in Learning: Realizing the Potential of American Higher Education.* Washington,

D.C.: Author. ED 246 833. 127 pp. MF–01; PC–06.

Nettles, M.T., and J.R. Johnson. 1987. "Race, Sex, and Other Factors as Determinants of College Students' Socialization." *Journal of College Student Personnel* 28: 513–24.

Newhouse, J.S., and A. McNamara. 1982. "The Transfer Student: A Dual Approach." *NACADA Journal* 2(1): 24–29.

Noble, J. 1988. "What Students Think about Academic Advising." In *The Status and Future of Academic Advising: Problems and Promise,* edited by W.R. Habley. Iowa City: American College Testing Program.

Noel, L., R. Levitz, D. Saluri, and Associates. 1985. *Increasing Student Retention.* San Francisco: Jossey-Bass.

O'Banion, T. 1972. "An Academic Advising Model." *Junior College Journal* 42(6): 62–64.

Okun, M.A., C.A. Kardash, W.A. Stock, I.N. Sandler, and D.J. Baumann. 1986. "Measuring Perceptions of the Quality of Academic Life among College Students." *Journal of College Student Personnel* 27: 447–51.

Overwalle, F.V. 1989. "Success and Failure of Freshmen at University: A Search for Determinants." *Higher Education* 18: 287–308.

Pascarella, E.T. 1980. "Student-Faculty Informal Contact and College Outcomes." *Review of Educational Research* 50: 545–95.

———. 1985. "College Environmental Influences on Learning and Cognitive Development." In *Higher Education: Handbook of Theory and Research,* vol. 4, edited by J.C. Smart. New York: Agathon Press.

Pascarella, E.T., and P.T. Terenzini. 1976. "Informal Interaction with Faculty and Freshman Ratings of Academic and Nonacademic Experience of College." *Journal of Educational Research* 70: 35–41.

———. 1978. "Student-Faculty Informal Relationships and Freshman Year Educational Outcomes." *Journal of Educational Research* 71: 183–89.

———. 1980. "Predicting Freshman Persistence and Voluntary Dropout Decisions from a Theoretical Model." *Journal of Higher Education* 51: 60–75.

———. 1981. "Residence Arrangement, Student/Faculty Relationships, and Freshman Year Educational Outcomes." *Journal of College Student Personnel* 22: 147–56.

Pascarella, E.T., P.T. Terenzini, and L. Wolfe. 1986. "Orientation to College and Freshman Year Persistence/Withdrawal Decisions. *Journal of Higher Education* 57: 155–75.

Patrick, J., J.W. Furlow, and S. Donovan. 1988. "Using a Comprehensive Academic Intervention Program in the Retention of High-Risk Students." *NACADA Journal* 8(1): 29–34.

Paulsen, M.B. 1989. "Developmental Academic Advising: Do Handicapped Advisors Have an Advantage?" *NACADA Journal* 9(2): 5–10.

Peterson, L., and E. McDonough. 1985. "Developmental Advising of Undeclared Students Using an Integrated Model of Student Growth." *NACADA Journal* 5(1): 61–69.

Petitpas, A., and D.E. Champagne. 1988. "Developmental Programming for Intercollegiate Athletes." *Journal of College Student Development* 29: 454–60.

Polson, C. 1986. "Advising Adult Learners." Paper presented at the National Conference on Academic Advising, October, Seattle, Washington. ED 277 902. 50 pp. MF–01; PC–02.

———. 1989. "Adult Learners: Characteristics, Concerns, and Challenges to Higher Education. A Bibliography." *NACADA Journal* 9(2): 86–112.

Polson, C.J., and W.E. Cashin. 1981. "Research Priorities for Academic Advising: Results of Survey of NACADA Membership." *NACADA Journal* 1(1): 34–43.

Polson, C.J., and J.P. Eriksen. 1988. "The Impact of Administrative Support and Institutional Type on Adult Learner Services." *NACADA Journal* 8(2): 7–16.

Pounds, A.W. 1989. "Black Students." In *The Freshman Year Experience: Helping Students Survive and Succeed in College,* edited by M.L. Upcraft, J.N. Gardner, and Associates. San Francisco: Jossey-Bass.

Purdy, D.A., S. Eitzen, and R. Hufnagel. 1982. "Are Athletes Also Students?" *Social Problems* 29(4): 439–48.

Raskin, M. 1979. "Critical Issue: Faculty Advising." *Peabody Journal of Education* 56: 99–108.

Remley, T.P., Jr., and R.O. Stripling. 1983. "Perceptions of Transfer Problems Experienced by Community College Graduates." *Journal of College Student Personnel* 24: 43–50.

Richardson, R.C., Jr., and L.W. Bender. 1987. *Fostering Minority Access and Achievement in Higher Education.* San Francisco: Jossey-Bass.

Richardson, R.C., Jr., and A.G. de los Santos, Jr. 1988. "From Access to Achievement: Fulfilling the Promise." *Review of Higher Education* 11: 323–28.

Richardson, R.C., Jr., H. Simmons, and A. de los Santos, Jr. 1987. "Graduating Minority Students." *Change* 19(3): 20–27.

Richter-Antion, D. 1986. "Qualitative Differences between Adult and Younger Students." *NASPA Journal* 23(3): 58–62.

Rudolph, F. 1962. *The American College and University: A History.* New York: Random House.

Russel, J.H., and T. Sullivan. 1979. "Student Acquisition of Career Decision-making Skills as a Result of Faculty Advisor Intervention." *Journal of College Student Personnel* 20: 291–96.

Ryan, F.J. 1989. "Participation in Intercollegiate Athletics: Affective Outcomes." *Journal of College Student Development* 30: 123–28.

Sagaria, M.A.D., L.C. Higginson, and E.R. White. 1980. "Perceived Needs of Entering Freshman: The Primacy of Academic Issues."

Journal of College Student Personnel 21: 243–47.

Saunders, S.A., and L. Ervin. 1984. "Meeting the Special Advising Needs of Students." In *Developmental Academic Advising: Addressing Students' Educational, Career, and Personal Needs,* edited by R.B. Winston, Jr., T.K. Miller, S.C. Ender, T.J. Grites, and Associates. San Francisco: Jossey-Bass.

Scherer, C., and N.S. Wygant. 1982. "Sound Beginnings Support Freshman Transition into University Life." *Journal of College Student Personnel* 23: 378–83.

Schubert, J.D., and G.W. Schubert. 1983. "Academic Advising and Potential Litigation." *NACADA Journal* 3(1): 1–11.

Sedlacek, W.E. 1987. "Black Students on White Campuses: 20 Years of Research." *Journal of College Student Personnel* 28: 485–95.

Shane, D. 1981. "Academic Advising in Higher Education: A Developmental Approach for College Students of All Ages." *NACADA Journal* 1(2): 12–23.

Shell, D.F., C.A. Horn, and M.K. Severs. 1988. "Effects of a Computer-Based Educational Center on Disabled Students' Academic Performance." *Journal of College Student Development* 29: 432–40.

Sloan, D., and M.B. Wilmes. 1989. "Advising Adults from the Commuter Perspective." *NACADA Journal* 9(2): 67–75.

Solomon, L.C., and B.J. Young. 1987. *The Foreign Student Factor.* New York: Institute of International Education.

Sowa, C.J., and C.F. Gressard. 1983. "Athletic Participation: Its Relationship to Student Development." *Journal of College Student Personnel* 24: 236–39.

Stage, F.K. 1989. "Reciprocal Effects between the Academic and Social Integration of College Students." *Research in Higher Education* 30: 517–31.

Stilwell, D.N., W.E. Stilwell, and L.C. Perritt. 1983. "Barriers in Higher Education for Persons with Handicaps: A Follow-up." *Journal of College Student Personnel* 24: 337–43.

Swift, J.S., Jr. 1987. "Retention of Adult College Students." *NACADA Journal* 7(2): 7–19.

Taylor, D.V., S.M. Powers, W.A. Lindstrom, and T.S. Gibson. 1987. "Academically Deficient Readmitted Students: Are They Really a High Risk?" *NACADA Journal* 7(1): 41–47.

Terenzini, P.T., and E.T. Pascarella. 1978. "Student-Faculty Informal Relationships and Freshman Year Educational Outcomes." *Journal of Educational Research* 71: 183–89.

———. 1980. "Student/Faculty Relationships and Freshman Year Educational Outcomes: A Further Investigation." *Journal of College Student Personnel* 21: 521–28.

Terenzini, P.T., E.T. Pascarella, and W.G. Lorang. 1982. "An Assessment of the Academic and Social Influences on Freshman Year Educational Outcomes." *Review of Higher Education* 5: 86–109.

Terenzini, P.T., C. Theophilides, and W.G. Lorang. 1984. "Influences on Students' Perceptions of their Academic Skill Development during College." *Journal of Higher Education* 55: 621–36.

Terenzini, P.T., and T.M. Wright. 1986. "Students' Academic Growth during Four Years of College." Paper presented at an annual forum of the Association for Institutional Research, June, Orlando, Florida. ED 280 420. 28 pp. MF–01; PC–02.

———. 1987. "Students' Personal Growth during the First Two Years of College." *Review of Higher Education* 10: 259–71.

Thomas, R.E., and A.W. Chickering. 1984. "Foundations for Academic Advising." In *Developmental Academic Advising: Addressing Students' Educational, Career, and Personal Needs*, edited by R.B. Winston, Jr., T.K. Miller, S.C. Ender, T.J. Grites, and Associates. San Francisco: Jossey-Bass.

Tinto, V. 1975. "Dropout from Higher Education: A Theoretical Synthesis of Recent Research." *Review of Educational Research* 45: 89–125.

———. 1987. *Leaving College: Rethinking the Causes and Cures of Student Attrition.* Chicago: Univ. of Chicago Press.

Tracey, T.J., and W.E. Sedlacek. 1985. "The Relationship of Noncognitive Variables to Academic Success: A Longitudinal Comparison by Race." *Journal of College Student Personnel* 26: 405–10.

Trombley, T.B. 1984. "An Analysis of the Complexity of Academic Advising Tasks." *Journal of College Student Personnel* 25: 234–39.

Trombley, T.B., and D. Holmes. 1981. "Defining the Role of Academic Advising in the Industrial Setting: The Next Phase." *NACADA Journal* 1(1): 1–8.

Uhl, N.P. 1983. "Institutional Research and Strategic Planning." In *Using Research for Strategic Planning*, edited by N.P. Uhl. San Francisco: Jossey-Bass.

U.S. Dept. of Education. 1985. *National Indicators of Education Status and Trends.* Washington, D.C.: National Center for Education Statistics.

Upcraft, M.L., J.N. Gardner, and Associates, eds. *The Freshman Year Experience: Helping Students Survive and Succeed in College.* San Francisco: Jossey-Bass.

Volkwein, J.F., M.C. King, and P.T. Terenzini. 1986. "Student-Faculty Relationships and Intellectual Growth among Transfer Students." *Journal of Higher Education* 57: 413–30.

Voorhees, R.A. 1990. "A Survey of Academic Advising as a Field of Inquiry." In *Higher Education: Handbook of Theory and Research,* vol. 6, edited by J.C. Smart. New York: Agathon Press.

Walsh, R.W. 1981. "Changes in College Freshmen Following Participation in a Student Development Program." Ed.D. dissertation, Texas Technical Univ.

Walter, L.M. 1982. "Lifeline to the Underprepared: Successful Academic Advising." *Improving University and College Teaching* 30(4):

159–63.

Walton, J.M. 1979. "Retention, Role Modeling, and Academic Readiness: A Perspective on the Ethnic Minority Student in Higher Education." *Personnel and Guidance Journal* 58(2): 124–27.

Watkins, B.T. 28 March 1990. "Consistent Information on Transfer Rates Sought for Community Colleges." *Chronicle of Higher Education:* A38.

Wilder, J.R. 1981. "A Successful Academic Program: Essential Ingredients." *Journal of College Student Personnel* 22: 488–92.

Williams, T.M., and M.M. Leonard. 1988. "Graduating Black Undergraduates: The Step beyond Retention." *Journal of College Student Development* 29: 69–75.

Wilson, R. 28 November 1990. "Foreign Students in U.S. Reach a Record 386,000." *Chronicle of Higher Education:* A1+.

Winston, R.B., S.C. Ender, and T.K. Miller, eds. 1982. *Developmental Approaches to Academic Advising.* New Directions for Student Services No. 17. San Francisco: Jossey-Bass.

Winston, R.B., T.K. Miller, S.C. Ender, T.J. Grites, and Associates, eds. 1984. *Developmental Academic Advising: Addressing Students' Educational, Career, and Personal Needs.* San Francisco: Jossey-Bass.

Winston, R.B. and J.A. Sandor. 1984. "Developmental Academic Advising: What Do Students Want?" *NACADA Journal* 4(1): 5–13.

Wiseman, R.L., R.A. Emry, and D. Morgan. 1988. "Predicting Academic Success for Disabled Students in Higher Education." *Research in Higher Education* 28: 255–69.

Wooldridge, H.W. 1982. "The Developmental Student: Advising Challenge of the 1980s." *NACADA Journal* 2(1): 8–12.

Wright, D.J. 1984. "Orienting Minority Students." In *Orienting Students to College,* edited by M.L. Upcraft. San Francisco: Jossey-Bass.

INDEX

A

Academic advising, 3
    as contributor to student success, 2
    delivery, 17
    students and learning, 2
Academic boredom, 43
Academic integration, 27, 43
    freshmen, 30
Academic performance
    African-American students, 27
    Hispanic students, 27
    student athletes, 34
    white students, 27
Academic planning, 15, 20
Academic support
    student athletes, 35
Academically underprepared students, 28, 44
ACT survey, 6, 7, 59, 60, 62, 67
Adjustment to college, 42, 44
    minority students, 27
Administrators
    suggestions for, 72
Adult students, 39, 53
    advising, 56
    definition, 54
    integration, 55
    long-term needs, 55
    motivation, 54
    short-term needs, 55
    time management, 55
Advisers
    as advocates. 39
    attitudes toward disabilities, 34
    effectiveness, 65
    evaluation, 59, 65, 66
    recognition, 65
    relationships to students, 64
    responsibilities, 64
    selection, 59, 63
    training, 59, 63, 64, 65
Advising
    adult students, 39
    as a process, 16
    freshmen students, 42
    institutional goals, 62
    international students, 38, 39
    mission, 61, 62

L

Learning disabilities
    advising students with, 33

M

Minority students
    achievement, 28
    adjustment to college, 27
    faculty contact, 27
    goodness of fit, 28
    retention and achievement, 26
Mission
    colleges and universities, 60
Motivating underprepared students, 30

N

National Academic Advising Association, 5, 6, 7
National Association of Academic Advisers for Athletics, 36
National Collegiate Athletic Association, 34
    academic guidelines, 35
National Institute of Education, 1, 2, 5
National Survey of Academic Advising, 3
Native Americans
    community colleges, 52
Nontraditional students, 53
Nonverbal communication skills, 29

P

Population diversity
    colleges, 24, 25
Positive college outcomes, 12
Prescribed curriculum, 3
Prescriptive advising, 15
Predictors of success, 28
Program management, 59

R

Reed College, 5
Rehabilitation Act of 1973, 31

S

Satisfaction with college, 13
Shared responsibilities
    students and advisers, 15
Social integration, 43
    freshmen, 30
Stages of assimilation, 42
Strategic planning, 60

Student athletes
 academic development, 34
 grade point average, 36
 persistence rates, 36
 personal development, 34
 social development, 34
 standardized test scores, 35
Student centered process, 4
Student-student collaboration, 68
Students
 achievement and advising, 45
 and adviser needs, 18, 23
 in transition, 39, 42
 integration into academic community, 2
 involvement in college, 9
 learning and personal development, 2
 success in college, 9
 with disabilities, 31
Support of students, 1
Supportive community
 in colleges, 26

T

Transfer counselors, 53
Transfer students, 39, 50
 academic orientation, 53
 contacts with advisers, 53
 retention, 51

U

Undecided students, 47, 48, 49, 50
UCLA Cooperative Institutional Research Program, 6
Urban Community College/Transfer Opportunities Program, 52, 53, 67

V

Verbal communication skills, 29

W

White student athletes,
 test scores, 35

ASHE-ERIC HIGHER EDUCATION REPORTS

Since 1983, the Association for the Study of Higher Education (ASHE) and the Educational Resources Information Center (ERIC) Clearinghouse on Higher Education, a sponsored project of the School of Education and Human Development at The George Washington University, have cosponsored the *ASHE-ERIC Higher Education Report* series. The 1991 series is the twentieth overall and the third to be published by the School of Education and Human Development at the George Washington University.

Each monograph is the definitive analysis of a tough higher education problem, based on thorough research of pertinent literature and insitutional experiences. Topics are identified by a national survey. Noted practitioners and scholars are then commissioned to write the reports, with experts providing critical reviews of each manuscript before publication.

Eight monographs (10 before 1985) in the ASHE-ERIC Higher Education Report series are published each year and are available on individual and subscription basis. Subscription to eight issues is $90.00 annually; $70 to members of AAHE, AIR, or AERA; and $60 to ASHE members. All foreign subscribers must include an additional $10 per series year for postage.

To order single copies of existing reports, use the order form on the last page of this book. Regular prices, and special rates available to members of AAHE, AIR, AERA and ASHE, are as follows:

Series	Regular	Members
1990-91	$17.00	$12.75
1988-89	15.00	11.25
1985-87	10.00	7.50
1983-84	7.50	6.00
before 1983	6.50	5.00

Price includes book rate postage within the U.S. For foreign orders, please add $1.00 per book. Fast United Parcel Service available within the contiguous U.S. at $2.50 for each order under $50.00, and calculated at 5% of invoice total for orders $50.00 or above.

All orders under $45.00 must be prepaid. Make check payable to ASHE-ERIC. For Visa or MasterCard, include card number, expiration date and signature. A bulk discount of 10% is available on orders of 15 or more books (not applicable on subscriptions).

Address order to
ASHE-ERIC Higher Education Reports
The George Washington University
1 Dupont Circle, Suite 630
Washington, DC 20036
Or phone (202) 296-2597
Write or call for a complete catalog of ASHE-ERIC Higher Education Reports.

1991 ASHE-ERIC Higher Education Reports

1. Active Learning: Creating Excitement in the Classroom
   Charles C. Bonwell and James A. Eison

2. Realizing Gender Equality in Higher Education: The Need to
   Integrate Work/Family Issues
   Nancy Hensel

1990 ASHE-ERIC Higher Education Reports

1. The Campus Green: Fund Raising in Higher Education
   Barbara E. Brittingham and Thomas R. Pezzullo

2. The Emeritus Professor: Old Rank - New Meaning
   James E. Mauch, Jack W. Birch, and Jack Matthews

3. "High Risk" Students in Higher Education: Future Trends
   Dionne J. Jones and Betty Collier Watson

4. Budgeting for Higher Education at the State Level: Enigma,
   Paradox, and Ritual
   Daniel T. Layzell and Jan W. Lyddon

5. Proprietary Schools: Programs, Policies, and Prospects
   John B. Lee and Jamie P. Merisotis

6. College Choice: Understanding Student Enrollment Behavior
   Michael B. Paulsen

7. Pursuing Diversity: Recruiting College Minority Students
   Barbara Astone and Elsa Nuñez-Wormack

8. Social Consciousness and Career Awareness: Emerging Link
   in Higher Education
   John S. Swift, Jr.

1989 ASHE-ERIC Higher Education Reports

1. Making Sense of Administrative Leadership: The 'L' Word in
   Higher Education
   Estela M. Bensimon, Anna Neumann, and Robert Birnbaum

2. Affirmative Rhetoric, Negative Action: African-American and
   Hispanic Faculty at Predominantly White Universities
   Valora Washington and William Harvey

3. Postsecondary Developmental Programs: A Traditional Agenda
   with New Imperatives
   Louise M. Tomlinson

4. The Old College Try: Balancing Athletics and Academics in
   Higher Education
   John R. Thelin and Lawrence L. Wiseman

5. The Challenge of Diversity: Involvement or Alienation in the
   Academy?
   Daryl G. Smith

6. Student Goals for College and Courses: A Missing Link in Assessing and Improving Academic Achievement
   Joan S. Stark, Kathleen M. Shaw, and Malcolm A. Lowther

7. The Student as Commuter: Developing a Comprehensive Institutional Response
   Barbara Jacoby

8. Renewing Civic Capacity: Preparing College Students for Service and Citizenship
   Suzanne W. Morse

1988 ASHE-ERIC Higher Education Reports

1. The Invisible Tapestry: Culture in American Colleges and Universities
   George D. Kuh and Elizabeth J. Whitt

2. Critical Thinking: Theory, Research, Practice, and Possibilities
   Joanne Gainen Kurfiss

3. Developing Academic Programs: The Climate for Innovation
   Daniel T. Seymour

4. Peer Teaching: To Teach is To Learn Twice
   Neal A. Whitman

5. Higher Education and State Governments: Renewed Partnership, Cooperation, or Competition?
   Edward R. Hines

6. Entrepreneurship and Higher Education: Lessons for Colleges, Universities, and Industry
   James S. Fairweather

7. Planning for Microcomputers in Higher Education: Strategies for the Next Generation
   Reynolds Ferrante, John Hayman, Mary Susan Carlson, and Harry Phillips

8. The Challenge for Research in Higher Education: Harmonizing Excellence and Utility
   Alan W. Lindsay and Ruth T. Neumann

1987 ASHE-ERIC Higher Education Reports

1. Incentive Early Retirement Programs for Faculty: Innovative Responses to a Changing Environment
   Jay L. Chronister and Thomas R. Kepple, Jr.

2. Working Effectively with Trustees: Building Cooperative Campus Leadership
   Barbara E. Taylor

1985 ASHE-ERIC Higher Education Reports

1. Flexibility in Academic Staffing: Effective Policies and Practices
   Kenneth P. Mortimer, Marque Bagshaw, and Andrew T. Masland

2. Associations in Action: The Washington, D.C. Higher Education Community
   Harland G. Bloland

3. And on the Seventh Day: Faculty Consulting and Supplemental Income
   Carol M. Boyer and Darrell R. Lewis

4. Faculty Research Performance: Lessons from the Sciences and Social Sciences
   John W. Creswell

5. Academic Program Review: Institutional Approaches, Expectations, and Controversies
   Clifton F. Conrad and Richard F. Wilson

6. Students in Urban Settings: Achieving the Baccalaureate Degree
   Richard C. Richardson, Jr. and Louis W. Bender

7. Serving More Than Students: A Critical Need for College Student Personnel Services
   Peter H. Garland

8. Faculty Participation in Decision Making: Necessity or Luxury?
   Carol E. Floyd

1984 ASHE-ERIC Higher Education Reports

1. Adult Learning: State Policies and Institutional Practices
   K. Patricia Cross and Anne-Marie McCartan

2. Student Stress: Effects and Solutions
   Neal A. Whitman, David C. Spendlove, and Claire H. Clark

3. Part-time Faulty: Higher Education at a Crossroads
   Judith M. Gappa

4. Sex Discrimination Law in Higher Education: The Lessons of the Past Decade. ED 252 169.*
   J. Ralph Lindgren, Patti T. Ota, Perry A. Zirkel, and Nan Van Gieson

5. Faculty Freedoms and Institutional Accountability: Interactions and Conflicts
   Steven G. Olswang and Barbara A. Lee

6. The High Technology Connection: Academic/Industrial Cooperation for Economic Growth
   Lynn G. Johnson

7. Employee Educational Programs: Implications for Industry and Higher Education. ED 258 501.*
Suzanne W. Morse

8. Academic Libraries: The Changing Knowledge Centers of Colleges and Universities
Barbara B. Moran

9. Futures Research and the Strategic Planning Process: Implications for Higher Education
James L. Morrison, William L. Renfro, and Wayne I. Boucher

10. Faculty Workload: Research, Theory, and Interpretation
Harold E. Yuker

1983 ASHE-ERIC Higher Education Reports

1. The Path to Excellence: Quality Assurance in Higher Education
Laurence R. Marcus, Anita O. Leone, and Edward D. Goldberg

2. Faculty Recruitment, Retention, and Fair Employment: Obligations and Opportunities
John S. Waggaman

3. Meeting the Challenges: Developing Faculty Careers. ED 232 516.*
Michael C.T. Brooks and Katherine L. German

4. Raising Academic Standards: A Guide to Learning Improvement
Ruth Talbott Keimig

5. Serving Learners at a Distance: A Guide to Program Practices
Charles E. Feasley

6. Competence, Admissions, and Articulation: Returning to the Basics in Higher Education
Jean L. Preer

7. Public Service in Higher Education: Practices and Priorities
Patricia H. Crosson

8. Academic Employment and Retrenchment: Judicial Review and Administrative Action
Robert M. Hendrickson and Barbara A. Lee

9. Burnout: The New Academic Disease. ED 242 255.*
Winifred Albizu Melendez and Rafael M. de Guzmán

10. Academic Workplace: New Demands, Heightened Tensions
Ann E. Austin and Zelda F. Gamson

*Out-of-print. Available through EDRS. Call 1-800-443-ERIC.

ORDER FORM

Quantity   **Amount**

_____ Please begin my subscription to the 1991 *ASHE-ERIC Higher Education Reports* at $90.00, 33% off the cover price, starting with Report 1, 1991   _____

_____ Please send a complete set of the 1990 *ASHE-ERIC Higher Education Reports* at $80.00, 41% off the cover price.   _____

_____ Outside the U.S., add $10 per series for postage   _____

Individual reports are avilable at the following prices:

1990 and forward, $17.00	1983 and 1984, $7.50
1988 and 1989, $15.00	1982 and back, $6.50
1985 to 1987, $10.00	

Book rate postage within the U.S. is included. Outside U.S., please add $1 per book for postage. Fast U.P.S. shipping is available within the contiguous U.S. at $2.50 for each order under $50.00, and calculated at 5% of invoice total for orders $50.00 or above. All orders under $45 must be prepaid.

PLEASE SEND ME THE FOLLOWING REPORTS:

Quantity	Report No.	Year	Title	Amount
			Subtotal:	
			Foreign or UPS:	
			Total Due:	

Please check one of the following:
- ☐ Check enclosed, payable to GWU-ERIC.
- ☐ Purchase order attached ($45.00 minimum).
- ☐ Charge my credit card indicated below:
  - ☐ Visa   ☐ MasterCard

Expiration Date _____

Name _____

Title _____

Institution _____

Address _____

City _____ State _____ Zip _____

Phone _____

Signature _____ Date _____

SEND ALL ORDERS TO:
ASHE-ERIC Higher Education Reports
The George Washington University
One Dupont Circle, Suite 630
Washington, DC 20036-1183
Phone: (202) 296-2597